# MARCO POLO

# TUSCANY

GERMANY
SWITZERLAND AUSTRIA
FRANCE
Milan
SLOVENIA
CROATIA
MC
Florence
RSM
BOSNIA-HERZEGOVINA
Corsica (F)
Tuscany
Rome
ITALY
Sardinia (I)
Naples
Ischia
Mediterranean Sea

www.marco-polo.com

# THE TOURING APP

shows you the way...
including routes and offline maps!

FREE!

# GET MORE OUT OF YOUR MARCO POLO GUIDE

IT'S AS SIMPLE AS THIS

**1** go.marco-polo.com/tus

**2** download and discover

# GO!

WORKS OFFLINE!

**SYMBOLS**

INSIDER TIP   Insider Tip

★   Highlight

🔘🔘🔘⚫   Best of...

🔆   Scenic view

♲   Responsible travel: for eco-
logical or fair trade aspects

(*)   Telephone numbers
that are not toll-free

**PRICE CATEGORIES
HOTELS**

*Expensive*   over 175 euros

*Moderate*   120–175 euros

*Budget*   under 120 euros

The prices are for two in a
double room per night in
peak season, including breakfast

**PRICE CATEGORIES
RESTAURANTS**

*Expensive*   over 30 euros

*Moderate*   20–30 euros

*Budget*   under 20 euros

Prices for a typical local main
dish with a vegetable side
dish and cover charge for
bread included

# CONTENTS

---

**MAPS IN THE GUIDEBOOK**
(142 A1) Page numbers and coordinates refer to the road atlas
(0) Site/address located off the map
Coordinates are also given for places that are not marked on the road atlas
(U A1) Coordinates for the city map of Florence inside the back cover
Maps of Siena and Pisa can be found on p. 62 and p. 98

(🔖 A–B 2–3) refers to the removable pull-out map

**INSIDE FRONT COVER:**
The best Highlights

**INSIDE BACK COVER:**
City map of Florence

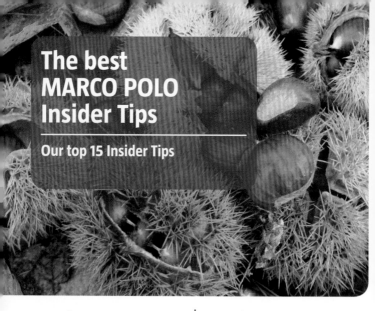

# The best MARCO POLO Insider Tips

## Our top 15 Insider Tips

**INSIDER TIP** **Slow shopping**

Promoting regionally sourced and sustainable products, *Unusualflorence* is also an advocate of the long since fashionable slow food movement → p. 38

**INSIDER TIP** **Historic baby hatch**

On 13 October 1445 at 5pm, the first baby was left in the foundling wheel under the arcades of the Florentine *Museo degli Innocenti.* → p. 35

**INSIDER TIP** **Nostalgic wine tour**

A wonderful way to explore the Tuscan countryside is with *organised day trips on a Vespa scooter* – take a relaxed ride through the flower-filled Chianti hills → p. 42

**INSIDER TIP** **Pistoia from below**

From oil press to mill wheel: Take a walk though the dark passages of *Pistoia Sotteranea* to understand the development of the ancient town → p. 44

**INSIDER TIP** **Forgotten river valley**

During the Middle Ages a lot more went on in the *Lunigiana,* in the extreme north-western tip of Tuscany, than today. This is set to change with the revival of the old Via Francigani that winds through the valley of the Magra River → p. 93

**INSIDER TIP** **Sustainable fishing**

The best way to honour a fish's death is by eating it – so goes the slogan of the Tuscany region to drum up publicity for virtually forgotten local types of fish, the so-called *pesce dimenticato* → p. 96

**INSIDER TIP** **Little Jerusalem**

At one time about 20 per cent of the residents of the small hill town of *Pitigliano,* in the south of Tuscany, were Jewish. Today there are not even enough to have a service, but their cultural heritage is maintained in an exemplary fashion → p. 78

**INSIDERTIP** Palio all year round

What few people know: The *Museum of Racehorses* in the Contrada L'Aquila in Siena is open to visitors on request → p. 60

**INSIDERTIP** Tuscan Caviar

Rock hard and amber colored: This exquisite delicacy is a specialty of the fishermen of the lagoon of Maremma: *Bottarga*, smoked mullet roe, delicious as a starter or grated over pasta → p. 78

**INSIDERTIP** Designer beds with a view

From suite No. 7 in *Palazzetto Rosso*, whose interior is a fusion of the modern and the medieval, you have a fantastic view over half of Siena. → p. 65

**INSIDERTIP** Heavenly beaches

Thanks to regional nature conservation, there are still untouched beaches like that of *Feniglia* on the Monte Argentario peninsula → p. 77

**INSIDERTIP** The scent of Prato

With poetic names like "Winter Breeze", *Wally's unique perfume creations*, all distilled according to ancient recipes, are not to be missed. You can find them in well stocked shops in Prato. → p. 49

**INSIDERTIP** Panoramic tours in public buses

Board the free beach shuttle *Navetta Spiagge* from Monte Argentario and enjoy the panoramic views on the beach road encircling almost the entire Island. → p. 78

**INSIDERTIP** The bread of the poor

From the forests of *Garfagnana* in Lucca's hinterland, manifold products made from chestnut flour make their way to the tables → p. 90

**INSIDERTIP** Truffle hunt

These hidden delicacies may defy the very best truffle hunters. But it is all about the hunt on this exciting walk in San Miniato. → p. 47

# BEST OF...

## FOR FREE

● *Vespa Museum*

In the *Museo Piaggio* in Pontedera, fans of the cult "wasp" scooters can immerse themselves in its history → p. 101

● *Art in the garden*

Rather than put his money in the bank, collector Giuliano Gori decided to invest in contemporary works by top-class artists and sculptors. The private collection is on display in his landscaped garden, *Fattoria Le Celle* at Pistoia. In the summer the garden is free of charge, but by appointment → p. 46

● *Combine bathing pleasure with cultural delights*

Remember to pack your bathing suit when you visit the Etruscan village of *Populonia.* There you can combine your cultural trip with a swim at the beach on the *Gulf of Baratti* – one of the most beautiful bays in the region, and there is no entrance fee → p. 83

● *Wellness for free*

The hot springs of *Saturnia* epitomise the wellness world. While hotel guests and day visitors stroll above in white terry cloth gowns, the sulphurous water cascades down into natural rock pools a few hundred feet below, enjoy them at no charge (photo) → p. 78

● *Princely splendour*

Amongst all the Medici villas around Florence, the *Poggio a Caiano* may well be the most beautiful and is certainly the most elegant → p. 41

● *Italian culture – for free*

From the Uffizi gallery, Palazzo Pitti or Bargello in Florence to the Pinacoteca Nazionale in Siena or the Archaeological Museum in Arezzo – admission is free to all *state museums* on the first Sunday in the month → p. 134

● *Picture-perfect Tuscany*

Churches and palazzi nestled behind high stone walls and narrow alleys that lead to atmospheric little squares: the picturesque *Cortona* is just as you imagined Tuscany to be → p. 58

● *The Cowboys of the Maremma*

The Italian Wild West of Tuscany: Men and women in wide-brimmed hats guard their cattle on horseback in the Maremma. The *butteri* (photo) demonstrate their riding prowess at the summer's many rodeos → p.74

● *In the Wine Country*

From the Supertuscans to honest table wine: What would a holiday in Italy be without its wonderful wines. The Chianti region between Florence and Siena is the wine country par excellence → p. 65

● *Agricultural cooperatives*

In the traditionally "red" Tuscany, farmers and local food producers work together and market their products in cooperative shops, like the *I Vini di Maremma* in Grosseto → p. 73

● *Culinary village festivals*

In the length and breadth of the area garish posters announce *sagras*. This is when the town square becomes a restaurant, with the women cooking local specialities and the men and children acting as waiters – and the proceeds mean that the soccer pitch gets a new surface → p. 126

● *Monastic hospitality*

Countless monasteries and pilgrim hospices offer affordable holiday accommodation, for instance *La Verna* in the Casentino and the Franciscan monastery *Domus Bernadiniana* at Massa Marittima → p. 58, 76

● *Engineers of the Iron Age*

The skills and the technical knowledge of the Etruscans deserve our admiration. More than two thousand years ago the lords of Maremma managed cut narrow paths and a complete necropolis into the soft volcanic rock in the southern Tuscan village of *Sovana* → p. 79

ONLY IN

# BEST OF...

● **Velvet and silk**
The city of Prato owes its fame and fortune to textile production. In the third millenium, they set up a themed *museum* which is housed in a converted textile factory → **p. 49**

● **Tuscan underworld**
Stalactite cave, copper mine, Etruscan tomb – an example: the cave labyrinth of *Grotta Antro del Corchia* at Carrara → **p. 93**

● **Fine chocolates and pralines**
Two or three of his pralines are enough to turn a rainy day into a happy day. An excellent reason for you to visit the shop of the Tuscan chocolate world champion, *Andrea Slitti*, in Monsummano Terme (photo) → **p. 46**

● **Remarkable collector**
During his lifetime the eccentric and eclectic Englishman and collector, Frederick Stibbert, turned his magnificent Florentine villa into a type of ethnographical *museum* where he lived amongst his remarkable collection of medieval knights, Japanese warriors, Chinese princesses and Indian maharajas → **p. 122**

● **The market hall in Livorno**
More than worth a visit not just on rainy days: You will be hard put to find a grander ambience in which to buy your fruit, greens and local delicacies than the lofty and ornate art nouveau hall of the *Mercato Centrale* in Livorno → **p. 81**

● **Carnival in Viareggio**
Since you are unlikely to visit Tuscany in the month of February, you can visit the *Museo del Carnevale* in Viareggio in order to see how the Tuscans celebrate carnival → **p. 96**

RAIN

# RELAX AND CHILL OUT
## Take it easy and spoil yourself

● *Divine harmony*
God was a Florentine! And you may well agree with the writer Anatole France, when you enjoy the sun and the panoramic view from the terrace of the *Piazzale Michelangelo* – look down over Florence and see how seamlessly the city and the surrounding nature blend into one another → **p. 32**

● *Relax after your sightseeing marathon*
Swollen feet and an aching back after your long walks and many hours of museums? Time for a wellness break – enjoy an aromatic shower, tropical shower or sauna in the *Hidron* just outside of Florence → **p. 38**

● *Refreshment for the soul*
Take a relaxing canoe trip in nature and glide along past unspoilt river banks with wild birds and grazing horses. This form of meditation ist made possible by *Maremma National Park* (photo) → **p. 75**

● *Pleasantly doing nothing*
In the comfortable chairs of the vegetarian restaurant *Essenza*, you can engage in *dolce far niente*, having a cup of tea and reading a book, chatting or listening to the live band in the evening – but you have to get up to sample the buffet → **p. 72**

● *Spa as a film backdrop*
Simply superb! With the mineral water treatment in the *Tettuccio Terme* in Montecatini you will not only purify your body – the magnificent environment, seen in numerous films, is a sight for sore eyes → **p. 46**

● *Getting there is half the fun*
Stroll downhill along the picturesque *Via Vecchia* in Fiesole towards Florence, which spreads itself out in the distance before you. Glorious villas and spacious parks line the way and depending on the time of year, the scent of jasmine, wine and lilies will be everywhere → **p. 41**

INTRODUCTION

# DISCOVER TUSCANY!

Is there such a thing as heaven on earth, a Garden of Eden where all your dreams come true? Well, Tuscany does come pretty close! The region is a veritable *cornucopia of surprises*, an Aladdin's cave that welcomes all who enter here. It is almost everything to every person: Romantics will find golden, rolling hills, a network of enchanted little villages and parks full of rippling fountains and fragrant rose walks. You can take leisurely tours in a horse and carriage, cruise *from vineyard to vineyard* on a Vespa or go paddling and bird watching on the rivers and lakes. What could be better than Tuscany in the summer, admiring the sunset and the sailing boats on the azure bays in your straw hat and silk scarf with a glass of the local red?

Too mellow for you? There is plenty of opportunity for derring-do in Tuscany: you can take the Angel Flight, the "volo dell'angelo" on a zip-line from one steep mountain top to another in the Apuan Alps or work up a sweat on the many *climbing and mountain bike routes* of the region. There is plenty of room at the top as the mountain ranges bordering Liguria and Emilia Romagna reach a height of more than 1000 metres. And afterwards, a relaxing evening workout in the *beach discotheques* on the coast to celebrate "la dolce vita".

Baptistery, cathedral and (leaning) campanile: the wonderful ensemble of Campo dei Miracoli in Pisa

Pilgrims at heart will find ecclesiastical splendour in the many cathedrals and the spirit of silence (and alcohol) in remote monasteries, taking it slowly along *the old pilgrimage route, the Via Francigena*, where the many tiny medieval churches offer rest and respite in their cool interior. You can take your camera on a discovery tour around the secret sites of Florence, take a dive in cool mountain rivers or spend a rare rainy day in a museum to rediscover the *inventions of Leonardo da Vinci*. Follow a truffle dog on the hunt for the largest truffle ever … well, all right, let's settle for a small one and a couple of chestnuts.

Artists and makers will feel right at home in the ateliers of the Tuscan artisans, who have been creating *intricate and beautiful things* for thousands of years. But where

to begin – in the quarries and the sculptors' workshops of the north or with a pottery or basket weaving class in an outdoor museum?

This brings us straight to the essence of Tuscany: *Art*! There are 500 museums, more than 3500 churches and 300 archaeological sites on an area roughly twice the size of Yorkshire. Art is everywhere – in Lucca, in Pisa, Livorno, Prato, Pistoia… and Florence basically IS art. In fact, the Tuscan capital is so full of art that there is a MARCO POLO travel guide just for Florence. Here, you can immerse yourself in a veritable ocean of paintings, patterns and shapes; statues that laugh, weep or even wrestle with each other, each one more life-like than the next. Since the Middle Ages, Florence has been a Mecca for artists: *Giotto, Giorgio Vasari, Leonardo da Vinci, Michelangelo* – they all came here and their traces can be found everywhere. For many centuries, Tuscans have made their mark not only on Italian society, but on Europe as a whole: Dante Alighieri is for Italy what Shakespeare is for Britain; both have made their respective languages, and their cultures, what they are today. Of course, Shakespeare's comedies tend to be more cheerful that Dante's "Divine Comedy"! And there are others, too: Think of Giovanni Boccaccio who wrote Europe's first novella collection, or Carlo Collodi, the creator of the famous wooden boy *Pinocchio*.

### Silence and spirits in remote monasteries

And there is even more art in Florence: Many local patrons commission sculptors to create artworks for their sumptuous private gardens; there is an entire *sculpture*

supported the Holy Roman Emperor)

**12th/13th century**
The establishment of the autonomous city republics

**1434**
Cosimo de' Medici seizes power and sets in motion a three hundred year long family hegemony, first in Florence but later also over the whole of Tuscany

**1737**
Tuscany falls to Habsburg-Lorraine

**1799–1815**
Napoleon's Tuscan intermezzo

**1860**
The nation votes to join the Kingdom of Sardinia

*garden* dedicated to Niki de Saint Phalle, the creator of the famous "Nanas," and not a day goes by where you cannot see a pavement artist kneeling on a Florence piazza and laboring for hours on end over a true masterpiece that will be washed away again in the evening. Well, art, after all, has been invented to come to terms with the ephemeral nature of life...

> **Acres and acres of vineyards shimmering in the heat of the sun**

Tuscany and *innovation* have been going hand in hand since the Etruscans settled here 3000 years ago, creating the first high culture of the region. Later, the Romans built flourishing merchant cities like Lucca and Florence, the places to be for the fashion victims of those bygone days. Tuscan philosophers, first and foremost Francesco Petrarca and his *humanism*, effectively ended the Middle Ages, while the rampant capitalism of today gave rise to the idea of *slow food* and Città slow, concepts made in Tuscany. Here, the participating villages concentrate on the production of quality over quantity, of improving the quality of life and reducing garbage to a minimum – quite a feat, given that most Italian cities are now literally drowning in rubbish.

This, of course, is another big plus for the region as a tourist destination. *Old chestnut forests* serve as noise absorbers, in the vast vineyards, you hear nothing but the faint sizzling of the summer's heat and the soft movements of the brushes on the amateur artists' canvases. Tourists practically disappear into the vast *nature reserves* with their acres and acres of fields where mouflons, horses, sheep and cattle graze.

The locals are well aware of the treasures they own and they seek to protect them through strict building and area protection regulations. For there is not much pristine, unspoiled nature left in Tuscany. Intense logging started already in Roman times and the dense deciduous forests gradually gave way to the now typical mixture of oak forests and *Mediterranean scrubland*, the macchia. The malaria infested swamps of the Maremma were recently drained and turned into fertile soil, which has given the region a new lease of life after hundreds of years of neglect. Now, farmers are selling their produce on the roadside. When it comes to tourism, Tuscany has truly learned from the mistakes of other regions: Here, they like to take things slow,

**1865–70**
Florence is the capital of the new Kingdom of Italy

**1944**
The German defence wall in the Apennines runs along the northern border of Tuscany, which thus becomes the battlefield

**1999**
Città Slow, a network for environmental protection and quality of life, is founded in Tuscany

**2017/2018**
In the second elections since the onset of the economic crisis the former mayor of Florence, Matteo Renzi, is seeking office again.
Tuscany addresses the crisis through investment in alternative energy and recycling.

eschewing the newest trends. Tuscany's almost *300 km of coastline* is an alternation of long, wide sandy beaches, sheltered pebble coves and rugged cliffs.

Tuscany is a treasure trove for unexpected culinary specialties: the wide saffron fields of the Florentine Chianti Region, Tuscan microbreweries, Tuscan cigars made in Lucca and the Valtiberina, and cowboys on powerful dark horses tending Longhorn cattle.

A festival of light: San Ranieri, Pisa's patron saint, is celebrated in June

Tuscans love to eat, and they stick together, whether playing against each other in the ancient football game of Calcio Fiorentino or in the world-famous Palio of Siena, a horse race in which the city districts compete against each other. There are also numberless sagras, *festivals dedicated to a local specialty*, where the locals proudly offer the best they have to those who come to visit.

**A perfect symbiosis of man and nature**

And the tourists love the taste of Tuscany – the soft nutty flavour of chestnut flour, the fragrance of hay, of sun on the vineyards, of truffles, saffron and prosciutto aged in marble basins and of cold, clear water. And there is hot water, too, because wellness is another Tuscan thing. For thousands of years, *thermal baths* have catered to every taste, from natural waterfalls near Saturnia to the ultra-posh thermal baths in Montecatini Terme. What can we say – complainers will have their work cut out!

# WHAT'S HOT

## 1 Splat, bang, pop

*Comics* Graphic novels are no longer just for children. Adult comics are true works of art and Italy's comic book capital lies in Tuscany. Not only does the Lucca Comics & Games festival take place here, it is also home to the *Museo Nazionale del Fumetto (Piazza San Romano 4)* comic museum. If you want to browse and buy, visit *Il Collezionista (Piazza San Giusto 1)*. In nearby Pescia, you will find *L'Elefante (Viale Europa 16)*, a library exclusively for comic books.

## Cin cin!

## 2

*Craft Beer* The Italians have always preferred beer with their pizza. Lately, young *birrifici* have even started to make their very own micro brews with a local touch of saffron or honey. Sampling the local craft beers for *aperitivo* has become quite the pastime, so expect lengthy queues, especially in De Cervesia *(Via Fillungo 92 | www.decervesia.it)* at the Porta dei Borghi in Lucca or the Vinile Lato B *(Via Beatrice 4)* in Massa.

## Workout on the water

## 3

*Core exercises* Windsurfers do it standing up – but on some days, there just isn't enough wind to swell the sails. Never mind, just swap a paddle for the sail and you are away on the latest craze: Stand-up-Paddling may be more Zen than vigorous action, but it is a super effective flab buster! Coastal Italians are doing it whenever they get the chance: on relaxed Sunday outings with friends and at dedicated SUP parties or competitions. You can rent a surfboard and paddle at every mountain lake, in the larger coastal resorts and on the Arno River in Florence.

# Street poetry

*Graffiti* "MeP D.25: The night flows like wine taking over our minds ..." In Florence, it is quite likely that you will be greeted with verses like these as you leave your house in the morning, possibly in large block letters on the opposite wall. You will find poems in all fonts and sizes, in a variety of languages, tacked to doors and lamp posts everywhere. "Liberate poetry!" is the rally cry of the bards hiding behind tags like G.70 or A.11. Meanwhile, the *Movimento per l'Emancipazione della Poesia* (MeP) has spread to other cities and many of its protagonists, it is said, have been located and invited to participate – under their real names – in such august occasions as the Festival di Letteratura Sociale in Florence. I wonder whether D.25 is one of them?

**4**

# Chilometro Zero

*Fresh from the field* "Vegetables from 0 kilometres away," claims the sign on the door. Well, all right, so the lupines may have travelled a few yards from the field to their final destination in the Bottega on the Piazza dei Mille in Livorno. But all the food served in Te Ke Voi in Siean is really ultra-local. And if Lara's supplier happens to be out of courgettes, there will be no zucchini risotto on the menu at Kmzero in Florence. The initiative *chilometro zero* started out as an online network of organic farms selling their produce on location. In the meantime, lots of restaurants have hopped on the bandwagon, because it just does not get any fresher, healthier and more sustainable than directly from the farm.

**5**

# IN A NUTSHELL

## THE NEW SPIRIT

At the end of the Middle Ages, Italy was sorely in need of a spiritual and artistic breath of fresh air. For far too long, the god-centric world view of the church had dominated every aspect of education, art and society as a whole. It is perhaps not surprising that the Renaissance began in unconventional Florence. The Florentine humanist poet Francesco Petrarca, critical of the overbearing, humorless and nitpicking papal doctrine, was instrumental in describing his own time as the "Dark Ages", as opposed to Classical Antiquity, which was then considered an era darkened by the absence of God. Petrarca called for living in the real world, joyfully and free of the dictum of the church. This gave rise to a new wave of art focusing on lifelike and dynamic representation; architects no longer built skywards to reach God but firmly championed the human, horizontal plane. As the Humanists sought inspiration in the classical ideals of art, science and philosophy, the painter and architect Giorgio Vasari called the new epoch Rinascita, "revival". By the 1600s, the new movement of Rinascimento, the Renaissance, which had started in Tuscany, had spread all over Europe.

## MEDIEVAL RAMBOS

Florence may be the go-to place for art and culture, but it can also raise a hell of a racket: Once a year, a bunch of testosterone-laden lads lay into each other at "calcio storico", a mixture of

**In Tuscany – home of the Renaissance – culture is everywhere; it is evident in every aspect of life, from cuisine to architecture**

modern rugby, soccer and wrestling. The objective is to get the ball into the opposite goal while 27 players team are trying to prevent this by pulling, pushing and beating the attackers. Attacks from behind and kicks to the head are the only moves that are forbidden. Small wonder then that concussions and bone fractures are the order of the day. Each game lasts for 50 minutes and the best of four teams will then play against each other in the finals on June 24 in front of the Church of Santa Croce. Back in the 15th century, the winning teams used to play right after mass, dressed in their Sunday best. Accordingly, the rules specifically state to this day that it is the prowess of the players and not the splendor of their garb that will determine who wins the game... The first prize is a capital banquet for everyone; back in the day, it was a prize cow shared, presumably, by the winning team!

# THE GOLDEN STUFF

Who would have thought that the humble purple flowers of the "saffron

In Sowana, a humble door hides a maze of splendid Etruscan tombs

crocus", a variety of the *Crocus sativus*, yield a harvest that is worth its own weight in gold for the saffron from the Val d'Orcia can fetch up to 35 euros per gram! But if you look at the labor involved, this seems more than fair, for to get one kilogram of saffron, you will have to hand-pick 200,000 flowers. The entire annual harvest of Italy only comes to a grand total of just about ten kilograms. You can barely make out the fragile flowers between the ancient olive groves and peaceful vineyards, but they are said to pack a medicinal punch: Saffron once used to be sprinkled on the bridal bed and on the bath water as an aphrodisiac. But take care: a little too much and you could die of incurable laughing fits. Today, saffron may still bring a smile to your face, for it is used mainly in wellness products or to add its unique color and flavor to honey and food.

# THE WATER MAN

Throughout his life, Dario Pinarelli had used a lot of water and produced a lot of waste water in his capacity as a chemist in the marble industry. But when the bubble burst, he lost his job. On the bright side, Dario and his new business partner are now all about water conservation and waste prevention. With the co-operation of local authorities, they set up garbage collection bins, educate school children and try to convince supermarkets and local communities to install free dispensers for drinking water. So far, they have been successful in Massa, Pietrasanta and Camaiore, where you can exchange used bottles for rebate points that can be redeemed in participating shops. This scheme also aims at boosting local trade and has been avidly adopted by the locals, who mostly redeem their points for food products.

# THE BERLUSCONIS OF FLORENCE

You could not get away from them even in the 15th century: The Medici, you might say, were the Berlusconi Clan of the Renaissance. The powerful merchant dynasty held sway in Florence and later all over Tuscany. They haggled, married and lynched their way up from humble peddlers to the bankers of the pope and later to several absolute monarchs. Except that their main passion was art, not football. Never without an ulterior motive, to be sure, for the Medici were merchants to the core. Always hungry for yet a little more power and wealth, they became famous patrons of the arts. Many artists lived and worked freely on a generous stipend. Small wonder then that back in the day, the city was teeming with artists and is positively bursting at the seams with master pieces (and their admirers) now.

## THE STOLEN TARTAN

Is it a case of cultural exchange or an early example of industrial espionage? Two nations puzzle over this conundrum and journalists, at least, consider it a case worth investigating. Preparing for an exhibition of medieval life in Siena, local archivists stumbled across several tartan patterns that predate everything that can be found in Scotland. Could it be that the pattern that appeared to have been the big thing in medieval Siena had been brought to Scotland afterwards? Certainly, the weavers of Lucca, Prato and environs were famous even back in the day. The question whether the Siennese went Scottish or the Scottish went Siennese may yet have diplomatic consequences...

## THE DEATH CULT OF THE PEACEFUL FEMINISTS

If you believe the archaeologists, the Etruscans must have been a happy people: There was peace and gender equality in Etruria and through the mining of the local iron ore the became skilled and wealthy artists and craftsmen. The Etruscans probably came to Italy from Asia Minor around 1000 BC, where they lived happily until the Romans came and took it all away. Now, all that is left of them are sumptuous funerary complexes full of grave goods of all kinds. You can find a particularly beautiful example of an Etruscan necropolis in the Archaeological Park of Sovana.

## WEED

Tuscany tickles your palate with a wealth of pleasures: wine, gelato, cakes and pastries, liqueurs, weed... Yes, we mean cannabis. It may not be strictly legal but it sure strikes a strong note in the fragrant summer evenings on the banks of the Arno or in the back streets of Massa and Pisa. Wherever you find young Italians, you will find weed. And since you are legally allowed to carry some on your person but are forbidden from selling it, Alessandro will sell you seeds, slug pellets, heat lamps or hemp oil and throw some weed in as a gift. Potheads come from far and wide to his shop in the village of Sarzana, and thousands of aficionados gather at the annual Canapisa Street Parade in Pisa to demonstrate for the legalization of cannabis. And, of course, to sing and to dance, for that is part of la *dolce vita*.

## CULT CIGARS

There once was, as the story goes, this oxcart full of Italian-grown tobacco that got all wet in a thunderstorm. The next day, the sun had come out again and the damp leaves began to ferment in the heat. This made the tobacco so strong that it is said three men are needed for a *Sigaro Toscano*: One man to smoke and two to hold him up. Well, so the local saying goes, but the members of the Toscano fan club pride themselves on smoking solo and Carlo Collodi, the author of Pinocchio, was likewise often seen to puff away unassisted. The manufacturers are seated in Mugnano near Lucca.

# FIFTY-FIFTY

Agricultural subsidy – sharecropping or *mezzadria* for the layman – was common in Italy from the Middle Ages until the land reform of the 1950s. It worked like this: The landowner loaned the land, the buildings and the livestock to the sharecropper, who did all the work and had to give half of his annual yield to him in payment. An easy life for the landowners, a hard slog for the peasants who constantly hovered on the brink of starvation. After the land reform, smallholders had the right to buy their farms, but hardly any of them had the means to do so. Most of them had no choice but to try their luck in the cities. This is the story behind the many abandoned farms in the hills of Tuscany. Initially, they were bought mostly by foreigners for holiday homes or rentals, but recently, there has been a new influx of Italian buyers.

# DOP & IGP

Intensive agriculture has never been a big thing in Tuscany, so there is a strong likelihood that the salami you can buy in the local market has come from happy pigs – but who really knows in today's global market? Do make sure to check the labels: IGP, Indicazione Geografica Protetta, can mean that the pork has come from Sicily and just received a local label. Instead, go for DOP *(Denominazione d'Origine Protetta)*, DOC *(Denominazione d'Origine Controllata)* or DOCG *(Denominazione d'Origine Controllata e Garantita)*. The ingredients used in these products are guaranteed to have been raised or grown in keeping with local tradition. Tuscan producers are trying to compete with the global market through short delivery distances and quality over quantity. Chestnut flower from the Garfagana, sheep's milk cheese from Pienza, wheat from Prato, Panforte from Sienna or the Prosciutto di Cinta Senese, a dry-cured ham from a Tuscan breed of domestic pigs are unmissable local delicacies that are best bought in small markets or farm shops.

# THE EMPEROR VERSUS THE CHURCH

Political strife is a traditional Italian pastime. In the 1200s, the main adversaries were the Guelfs and the Ghibellines – the former faithful to the pope, the latter to the emperor. Today you would place them left and right of the centre. Caught in the middle of this were independent city states like Florence, Lucca and Pisa.

Small cities lived dangerously in the midst of all these power struggles and needed strong allies. Hence, Florence and Lucca sided with the pope, for the church was well connected internationally, which is good for trade. Arezzo, Pisa and Siena threw in their lot with the Hohenstaufen emperor who welcomed anyone who helped him stand up to the power-hungry Medici of Florence. But now, things were getting complicated: The church, rather progressively for its time, wanted the "upstarts", the wealthy merchants of the cities, to have a say in politics, while the royal Ghibellines strove to keep the power with the emperor. The people, however, were putting their political alignment over their own local interests – so the Ghibelline Florentines fought for Siena and the Guelph Siennese fought for Florence. Are you with me? And even now, "guelfi" and "ghibellini" are often used as monikers for the political Left and Right.

## TAKE IT EASY

Amid the general hysteria of "higher, faster, further" it was about time for the rediscovery of slowness. And where better than in Tuscany? So the mayor of Greve in Chianti came up with the idea of *città slow*, the slow city. You can pick them out amidst the network of picturesque Tuscan villages, for they are even more quaint, clean, and even more alive. Here, you can buy local specialties in small *botteghe* and browse the shops of artists and artisans. Here, the entire community works together as a tight-knit team, organising local fetes and maintaining the village. And it is far easier to get ahead in foot or by bicycle in places like Greve, Barga or Capalbio, for you have to leave the car outside the village. There are more than a dozen "slow cities" in Tuscany, but for this, they had to meet strict criteria (www.cittaslow.it): Sustainability over mass tourism, a respect for nature over industrialism, a spirit of hospitality and quality of life are a must.

## MEDITERRANEAN JUNGLE

Apart from the various and very distinctive species of conifers, the *macchia* – a low, impenetrable scrubland of laurel, gorse, junipers, arbutus, tree heath, rosemary and myrtle – is probably the most recognizable landscape feature of the Mediterranean. Hence, it also gives the Tuscan landscape its characteristic appearance. But this was not always so: In antiquity, the whole region was densely forested. Then, the Etruscans came and after them, the Romans, and they cut down the trees to fire their stoves, their public baths and their glass and metal-working furnaces. The logging, unhampered by any kind of foresight, went on well into the Middle Ages and in time, the now naked and barren landscape fell victim to soil erosion. In time, these areas were taken over by the hardy and fragrant evergreen shrubs that can easily withstand the dry heat of the summer.

Yummy! Charcuterie products from the Cinta-Senese pigs of Tuscany

# FOOD & DRINK

The guiding principle of traditional Tuscan cuisine is to use only a few ingredients but they need to be of the very best quality. The food is not overly refined; the emphasis is rather on the taste of each separate ingredient in the dish.

Tuscan cuisine uses fresh regional produce – a *rural cuisine* where whatever is found seasonally in the garden, stable or forest, is served at the table. The most important ingredient is *cold pressed olive oil*. In Tuscany the much vaunted light Mediterranean diet is the most natural thing in the world. The ⊗ labels "Vetrina Toscana" and "Campagna Amica" are synonymous with sustainably farmed and sourced produce.

Antipasto, *primo, secondo,* dessert: eating all the dishes does not happen that often in Tuscany anymore. Nowadays it happens when people have guests over, when friends and colleagues meet up in restaurants or on festive days when the whole family is gathered around the table. Meals are always accompanied by bottles of *acqua minerale*, either *liscia* (still) or *gasata* (with gas), local red wine *(vino di casa)* and bread made without salt. Because with all the *aromatic herbs* and fresh flavours, you do not need any salt.

For *prima colazione* (breakfast), pastries and coffee are preferred, usually in the bar on the corner so avoid the boring breakfast buffet in the hotel and do as the locals do but remember to only order

Photo: *crostini* with sun-dried tomatoes

Top quality, fresh basic ingredients are the cornerstone of Tuscany's delicious – and healthy – cuisine

an *espresso con latte caldo* or cappuccino – or else you will be served instant coffee *(caffè americano)* as a caffè latte. **Antipasti** are meant to keep guests happy while they wait for the freshly prepared meal. Typical in Tuscany are *crostini* or bruschetta with vegetables pickled in oil, *prosciutto* with melon or a *pinzimonio,* mixed raw vegetables with olive oil. This is followed by the *primo piatto*, the first course, usually pasta or, typically in Tuscany, a **hearty vegetable soup**. The main course, the *secondo*, consists of fish or meat and a salad or vegetable side dish *(contorno)* if desired. This is rounded off with fruit, sheep's milk cheese or *cantuccini*, hard almond biscuits from Prato, which are dunked in the *vin santo* dessert wine.

If you love ice cream, you will be in heaven as there are *gelateria* everywhere in Tuscany. Look for the *artigianale* (home made) sign and watch out if the ice cream is piled high as that is a sure sign that it contains all sorts of additives.

# LOCAL SPECIALITIES

aglio, olio, peperoncino – minced garlic and chillies in cold pressed olive oil – unbeatable as a pasta sauce

arista alla fiorentina – roast pork, seasoned with garlic and rosemary

arista alla fiorentina – T-bone steak (the best is Chianina beef from the Chiana region). The meat is cooked on a charcoal grill and then seasoned and brushed with olive oil

bollito con salsa verde – mixed cooked meat (chicken, beef, tongue ...) with a sauce made from herbs and olive oil

bruschetta – toasted white bread brushed with garlic, salt, olive oil and eventually tomato

cacciucco alla livornese – creamy fish soup made from everything that the sea has to offer

castagnaccio – cake made from chestnut flour with pine nuts and rosemary

crostini – toasted white bread, often with chicken liver pâté (photo left)

fagioli all'uccelletto – white beans in tomato sauce with sage

panforte/panpepato – spiced Christmas cake with almonds and candied fruit – from Siena (photo right)

pappa col pomodoro – a primo of tomato sauce and stale bread

peposo – Tuscan veal stew with lots of black pepper and red wine

pici – thick durum wheat noodles, good with a hearty meat sauce

pinzimonio – carrots, fennel, celery sticks dipped raw in a mixture of olive oil and salt

ribollita – soup of white beans, cabbage and soup vegetables, best eaten reheated ("ribollita")

trippa alla fiorentina – veal tripe with tomato sauce and soup vegetables

zuppa di farro – spelt soup with soup vegetables and kale

In tourist centres, fixed price menus (menú turistico) are often on offer but if you prefer not to have a set menu, you will need to spend a little more. In addition there is the coperto, a flat charge for cover and bread.

The servizio, a service charge, is usually included in the price of the meal. Tips are only given if you are satisfied with the service. The distinctions between the **different types of restaurants** – ristorante, trattoria, osteria, pizzeria, rosticceria, enoteca – are often blurred and the different price categories are of no help either. If you want to avoid any uncomfortable surprises it is best to first check the menus that are posted outside the restaurant.

There are bars on almost every corner where locals start the day with a cappuccino and a *brioche*, a croissant or other types of sweet pasty. In the afternoons they serve sandwiches (*panini* or triangular *tramezzini*) with salad and at night you can enjoy an *aperitivo*. Although the drinks might be more expensive at this time, you may however, enjoy the *finger food buffet* for free while the *pasticcerie* has the cakes and pastries that guests often take along to evening dinner invitations.

52 DOP (eleven DOCG, 41 DOC) and six IGP: this is how Tuscany promotes its wine industry. The region tops the list of Italian *quality wines* that have the controlled seal of approval. And that is only the tip of the iceberg – or rather the vineyard – because in the over 40 cultivated regions, some top wines like the Sassicaia (one of the legendary prizewinning „*Super Tuscans*") hide behind the *vino da tavola* category. A tip if you are uncertain: look for *prodotto e imbottigliato all'origine* on the label, this means that the wine was bottled by the grower and the vintner uses his name as a guarantee of quality.

Tuscany traditionally produces red wines, Brunello di Montalcino, Vino Nobile di Montepulciano, **Chianti Classico** and Morellino di Scansano are the bestsellers of the region. They all have one thing in common, the Sangiovese grape, the Tuscan grape par excellence.

However, white wines are also very popular, especially the dry and fruity Vernaccia di San Gimignano from another *typically Tuscan grape variety*. In general, the other grapes grown in the region have come from elsewhere, like Merlot, Cabernet Sauvignon or the famous Sardinian white wine variety Vermentino, the current star of the Tuscan white wines.

The sweet *vin santo* is an excellent Tuscan **dessert wine**. The white grapes are hung in a well ventilated room, dried and stored for at least three years before use.

A perfect match: *cantuccini* and *vin santo*

# SHOPPING

For some shopping is the best medicine. And there is no better place than Tuscany to indulge in some retail therapy, after all it has a long tradition of great style and artistic flair. Here comes an A to Z to shopping in Tuscany.

## ACCESSORIES

Italian elegance is very evident in the small things: the refined scarf, the gorgeous hat, the hand crafted shoes, the unusual costume jewellery, and embroidered napkins for the festive table. The stylish Tuscans are surrounded by beauty and they know exactly what fits best with what. If you can afford it, it is best to purchase your accessories either from a traditional speciality shop or from one of the luxury boutiques of the top international fashion designers. However, you can be very creative even with a modest budget: look in the the local *mercerie* (haberdashery) stores, as well as in the large department stores like Coin, La Rinascente or Upim and sometimes even on the rummage tables at the weekly market. All you need here is just a bit more time.

## CULINARY

Every area, and almost every village, in Tuscany has its own culinary speciality: chestnut flour from Garfagnana, *lardo* (bacon fat) from Colonnata in the Apuan Alps cured in marble vats, pecorino from Pienza, chocolates from Monsummano Terme... these are the travel souvenirs most popular with Italians. Thus, you need never look very far, not even in the most remote corner, for a delicatessen or farming cooperative that makes or sells these tasty culinary souvenirs. Even the large supermarket chains, such as Coop, now have sections that feature the region's specialties. One of the real success stories of the region is the Campagna Amica, the marketing initiative of the regional farmers' markets, where the vegetable farmers, shepherds and livestock farmers of the surrounding area offer their produce on the weekends. You can also buy regional wine in wine shops *(enotece)* and *vino sfuso* in the smaller shops and of course directly from the producers, but bear in mind that the unsealed *vino sfuso* does not travel well.

Tuscany is the source of many fine things –
buy yours at the farmer's market, the *enoteca*,
the department store or the outlet centre

## CRAFTWORK

*Arte* and *arti* – art and handcraft – in the Italian language, these are two sides of the same coin and the region of Tuscany has been famous for centuries for its skillful workmanship of the most varied materials – leather, paper, and terracotta, gold, marble and straw. These old skills have been handed down from generation to generation and in addition to the traditional crafts – picture frame gilding, making mosaics and hand painting ceramics – you can also choose from a plethora of contemporary crafts that combine tradition with the spirit of the times. In small boutique workshops, *botteghe*, Tuscan masters still create their masterpieces today and it is really worth spending the time to watch them while they work. When you see the care and skill they put into their craft, you will understand that quality has its price.

## FASHION & MARKETS

Milan had, for a long time, replaced Florence as fashion capital. Yet it was Tuscan labels such as Gucci, Pucci, Prada and Ferragamo that made Italian fashion famous. But the city on the Arno is catching up again and Tuscan creativity is once again at the forefront. Everywhere young stylists are setting up their own studios and making limited edition items, the fashion streets in the Tuscan city centres are always right on trend with the latest fashions – and often a season ahead of other European cities. If you cannot afford the alta moda, you need only be a little patient. At the end of the season the creations are sold off at the weekly markets or in one of the many outlets that are often conveniently situated next to motorway exits, or on the outskirts of town, and are places of pilgrimage for families during weekends.

# FLORENCE & THE NORTH

As diverse as the three provinces of the north-east are – Florence rooted in its past, commercial Prato and peaceful Pistoia – together they form the political and economic centre of Tuscany. Their wealth has come through trade and workmanship, their fame through art, culture and a unique garden landscape.

## FLORENCE (FIRENZE)

▨▨▨ **MAP INSIDE BACK COVER**
(146 C6) *(ØJ J–K8)* **During 1817,** the French writer Stendhal wrote a travel article in which he warned that Florence

**CITY** **WHERE TO START?**
The ● ⚓ **Piazzale Michelangelo (U E6)** is the perfect place to take in the beauty and harmony of the city. The stress free option is to take bus 13 from the station, since the inner city is closed to car traffic. A stairway leads you from there down to the Oltrarno, the part of the city on the left bank of the Arno that is full of craft workshops. From there you can go over the famous Ponte Vecchio bridge, into the city centre with its famous landmarks; the Palazzo Vecchio, the Duomo and the Basilica Santa Croce.

Urban landscapes as works of art: in and around Florence, Prato and Pistoia, beauty and quality of life are very much at home

can make you ill – this was after he collapsed here from sheer art exhaustion. During the 20th century a Florentine psychiatrist diagnosed this reaction as the "Stendhal Syndrome" when dozens of visitors to Florence suffered a similar reaction.

And indeed there is nowhere else where you will find so much art in such a small area than in this city (pop. 377,000) where, in the 14th century, the Renaissance heralded a new age of philosophy, art and architecture. Not only is it an open air museum but it is also a city of shopkeepers and craftsmen. During the day the city is full of the sounds of artisans hammering and sawing in workshops. During the evening the city is also alive, as bars and restaurants put their tables out in the street and fun lovers travel from the one venue to the next. This travel guide only covers the essentials on Florence. For detailed information, consult the MARCO POLO "Florence" guide.

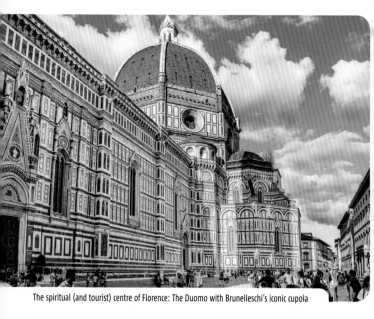

The spiritual (and tourist) centre of Florence: The Duomo with Brunelleschi's iconic cupola

## SIGHTSEEING

### CATHEDRAL, BAPTISTERY AND CAMPANILE (U C3)

You almost except to spy "the hunchback of the Duomo" or perhaps the "phantom of the Cattedrale Santa Maria del Fiore" among the parapets, cupolas and secret doors of Florence cathedral. The atmosphere is truly mystical. On the day of the summer solstice, the light filtering through a small hole in the cupola hits the spot exactly in the centre of the circle on the floor beneath. The splendid byzantine mosaic on the ceiling of the hexagonal *Battisterio di San Giovanni* is a must-see. Although the baptistery was consecrated in 1509, its roof remained open for 150 years until Filippo Brunelleschi closed it with a self-supporting ★ ☽ cupola. ☽ Giotto's bell tower, the *campanile*, had long been finished at that time. Much of the cathedral's artwork is now in the museum *dell'Opera del Duomo* nearby, for instance Donatello's penitent Mary Magdalen, Michelangelo's Pietà and the paradise door by Lorenzo Ghiberti. *Cathedral Mon–Wed and Fri 10am–5pm, Sat 10am–4.45pm, Sun 1.30pm–4.45pm, Thu 10am–4pm, July–Sept 10am–5pm; baptistery Mon–Fri 8.15am–10.15am and 11.15am–7.30pm, Sat 8.15am–7.30pm, 1st Sat of the month 8.15am–2.45pm and 5.15pm–7.30pm, Sun 8.15–14.45; cupola Mon–Fri 8.30am–7pm, Sat 8.30am–5pm, Sun 1pm–4pm; campanile daily 8.15am–7.20pm; museum daily except 1st Tue of the month 9am–7pm | combined ticket for all 5 monuments 15 euros | www.ilgrandemuseodelduomo.it*

### GALLERIA DELL'ACCADEMIA (U D2)

This is where you will find the star of the history of art – Michelangelo's David (the sculpture on the Piazza della Signoria is only a copy) – with the famed head wreathed in ivy and the proud muscular body. But there are many more high-calibre works of art on show here. Advance booking is recommended *(4 euros | tel. 0 55 29 48 83)*. *Tue–Sun 8.15am–6.50pm | 8 euros | Via Ricasoli 60 | www.galleriaaccademiafirenze.beniculturali.it*

### GALLERIA DEGLI UFFIZI ★ (U C4)

In 1560 Cosimo I de' Medici assigned this u-shaped building for the officials of the Republic of Florence. The art gallery was constantly enlarged. Today the Medici's cultural and artistic legacy takes up 45 of its rooms. Included are Sandro Botticelli's *Allegory of Spring*, Leonardo da Vinci's *Annunciation* and Filippo Lippi's *Depictions of Mary*. Advance booking recommended *(4 euros | tel. 0 55 29 48 83)*. *Tue–Sun 8.15am–6.50pm | 8 euros | Piazzale degli Uffizi 6 | www.uffizi.firenze.it*

### INSIDER TIP MUSEO DEGLI INNOCENTI (U D3)

The babies depicted on the terracotta medallions on the exterior façade of the Della Robbia reveal the purpose of the building as Italy's oldest foundling hospital (now a museum). Built in 1445 by Filippo Brunelleschi the building was a front-runner of the horizontal building style of the Renaissance. *Daily 10am–7pm | 7 euros | Piazza della Santissima Annunziata 12 | www.istitutodeglinnocenti.it*

### MUSEO NOVECENTO (U B3)

Yes, really – there is art after the renaissance! Here, in fact, you can see more than 300 video installations, sculptures and paintings showcasing what 20th century artists were all about. They were, in a word, out to shock. Take a tour through the beginnings of catwalk shows

## MARCO POLO HIGHLIGHTS

★ **Galleria degli Uffizi in Florence**
Visit the stars in the 45 room Hall of Fame of Italian painting: da Vinci, Botticelli, Michelangelo, Raffael are all there - with friends! → p. 35

★ **Cathedral dome in Florence**
Filippo Brunelleschi's imposing *cupola*: an architectural marvel and a structural engineer's dream! → p. 34

★ **Montecatini Terme**
A nostalgic and charming art nouveau spa town → p. 46

★ **Museo del Ricamo in Pistoia**
See generations of craftsmanship in the Embroidery Museum → p. 44

★ **Museo Novecento in Florenz**
A place where art makes you stop and think. → p. 35

★ **Palazzo Pitti in Florence**
Splendour and art in the Medici residence → p. 36

★ **Medici Villas**
For the first time a reign was presented as festive and serene, different from the Middle Ages → p. 41

★ **San Zeno Cathedral in Pistoia**
The silver altar is a medieval masterpiece! → p. 44

★ **Santo Stefano Cathedral in Prato**
A masterpiece of Tuscan craftsmanship → p. 49

in the 1950s, poetry collages and visual sound experiments and have a look at the film hall, where Florence is featured in a collection of film clips from the romantic to the avantgarde. *April–Sept Sat–Wed 11am–8pm, Thu 11am–2pm, Fri 11am–11pm, Oct–March Fri–Wed 11am–7pm, Thu 11am–2pm | 8.50 euros | Piazza Santa Maria Novella 10 | www.museo novecento.it*

### PALAZZO PITTI AND
### GIARDINO DI BOBOLI (U B5–6)

During the 15th century the merchant Luca Pitti wanted to build the largest palace in the city on the left side of the river. He went bankrupt and had to watch as his worst enemies, the Medici family, built the ⭐ *Palazzo Pitti* up to its current size. The palace houses six museums, including the picture gallery *Galleria Palatina (Tue–Sun 8.15am–6.50pm | 8.50 euros | Piazza Pitti 1)*. Behind it lie the *Boboli Gardens (April/May/Sept/Oct daily 8.15am–6.30pm, June–Aug 8.15am–7.30pm, Nov–March 8.15am–4.30pm, closed 1st and 4th Mon | 7 euros)* which were laid out in 1550. The gardens have ornamental gardens, cool grottoes and pergolas. Entrance ticket for all museums: 11.50 euros, valid for three days.

### PALAZZO VECCHIO (U C4)

For 700 years, the fortress-like Palace at the Piazza della Signoria has been the focus of Florence's secular power. Do visit the Salone dei Cinquecento, a magnificent hall covered in frescoes. *Fr–Wed 9am–7pm, April–Sept until 11pm, Thu 9am–2pm | 10 euros, Tower +10 euros, combined ticket 14 euros | museicivicifiorentini. comune.fi.it*

### PONTE VECCHIO 🜋 (U C4–5)

The bridge, with its three stone arches and its pastel coloured buildings, links the two banks of the Arno where trade flourished during the Middle Ages. Running above the shops is *Vasari's Corridor*, build so that the Medicis could move freely between their office rooms and the Palazzo Pitti.

### SAN LORENZO
### AND CAPPELLE MEDICEE (U C3)

An effective if rather pricey way to be remembered: The fabulously wealthy and powerful Medici asked the best artist of their day – no other than Michelangelo Buonarotti – to build two ornate chapels over their family graves. *You can visit the Medici Chapels daily 8.15am–5pm; 1st/3rd/5th Mon and 2nd/4th Sun closed. | 8 euros | www.polomuseale.firenze.it.* With the old sacristy created by Filippo Brunelleschi, Donatello's pulpits and the fabulous marble mosaics in the Chapel, there is such an abundance of riches in the Basilica di San Lorenzo that you will hardly know where to look first. *(Mon–Sa 10am–5pm, March–Oct also Sun 1.30–5.30pm | 6 euros | Piazza di San Lorenzo).*

### SANTA CROCE ⭐ (U D4)

In the late Middle Ages, blue pigment was as valuable as gold. But this did not deter the painter Giotto: His paintings are a riot of tangible, life-like characters full of human emotions on a background resplendent with ultramarine blue. No wonder that he is considered one of the pioneers of the renaissance! *Mon–Sat 9.30am–5pm, Sun 2–5pm | 6 euros | Piazza di Santa Croce 16 | www.santacroceopera.it*

## FOOD & DRINK

### TRATTORIA LA CASALINGA (U B5)

The name says it all: here you get typical Tuscan home cooking – tripe, bread soup, boiled meats – at moderate prices. But the word is out – so now you may have to wait awhile in the evenings for a free table. *Closed Sun | Via dei Michelozzi 9r | tel. 0 55 21 86 24 | www.trattoriacasalinga.it| Moderate*

### KMZERO BISTROT  (U E4)

Lara's excellent cuisine is created exclusively from the finest locally produced ingredients: If it is not in season, you will not find it on the menu! *Daily | Piazza Lorenzo Ghiberti 20–21 | tel. 34 88 75 43 43 | Budget–Moderate*

### INSIDER TIP PUNTO CAMPAGNA AMICA (U D4)

In this quaint medieval building with its wooden gallery, you can sit down for a hearty meal or buy panini to go – everything made from organic ingredients and moderately priced. *Tue/Wed 10am–8pm, Thu–Sat 10am–10pm | Via Matteo Palmieri 25r | tel. 39 22 79 26 63 | Budget–Moderate*

### LO SCHIACCIAVINO (U D4)

In their *paninoteca* Vale and Leo specialise in the yeast flatbread *schiacciata* (spoken "scjatchata") filled with local Tuscan sausage and cheese specialties. *Closed Mon evening, in August also Sun | Via Ver-*

di 6r | tel. 05 52 26 0133 | www.facebook.com/schiacciavino | Budget*

## SHOPPING

### FIERUCOLA (U B5)

On the third Sunday of the month, Florentines spoil themselves with organic products from the surrounding region at this farmer's market. *9am–7pm | Piazza Santo Spirito | www.lafierucola.org*

### LADY JANE B. (U E3)

We guarantee that you will leave this place a changed woman! The tiny, quirky boutique is usually filled to the rafters with happy customers and friends and of course with the finest vintage outfits and accessories, sourced by the creative owner Sabry or designed and made by herself. From elegant to out there, you will find everything to suit your sartorial fancy and the prices are more than correct. *Via dei Pilastri 32b*

### FASHION

Names like Gucci, Ferragamo, Cavalli, Pucci, Patrizia Pepe and Prada are all testimony to Tuscan elegance and their luxury bou-

Pomp and circumstance in the Palazzo Vecchio: Cortile Michelozzo

tiques are in *Via Tornabuoni, Via della Vigna Nuova* and *Via Roma* (U B–C 3–4) while areas like Santa Croca and Santo Spirito are the domains of the smaller labels like *Mimi Furaha* (U D4) *(Borgo degli Albizi 35r | www.mimifuraha.it)* or *Flo Concept Store* (U B4) *(Lungarno Corsini 30–34r | www.flo-firenze.org)*.

## SIMONE TADDEI (U C4)

His calf's leather photo frames and cigarette cases go through about 30 steps until they look as though they are made from wood. *Via Santa Margherita 11*

**INSIDER TIP** UNUSUALFLORENCE ⊙

*Amblé* has the ambiance of a very colourful flea market, for *Irene* specializes in vintage furniture and clothing. Here, you can enjoy an excellent cup of organic coffee while hunting for a quirky bargain to update your home. Choose from a collection of original perfumes at *AquaFlor* – or learn how to make it yourself in one of the many workshops. Longing for a new outlook on life? *I Visionari* are the specialists for spectacular spectacles. The 17 "unusual" businesses that have come together here represent the Florentine cutting edge in creativity, quality and sustainability. You can pick up a map for a self-guided walk around these venues at the tourist office and at *unusualflorence. blogspot.com*.

## SPORTS & ACTIVITIES

Raring to get on your bike? Fetch yourself a map from *Florence by bike* (U C2) *(Via San Zanobi 54r | tel. 0 55 48 89 92 | www. florencebybike.it)* or just follow the path along the river Arno. Or just take five on the city beach *Spiaggia sull'Arno* am *Lungarno Serristori* (U D5) – after all, you are on a holiday! If your feet can't take all that culture anymore, treat yourself

to a relaxing massage at ● Hidron FunSport (146 B5) *(ᗪ J7) (Via di Gramignano | Campi Bisenzio | www. hidron.it)*, Italy's biggest wellness centre a few kilometres outside of Florence. Literary thrill seekers can follow the footsteps of Dan Brown's Hero Robert Langdon into the abyss of human depravity and Christian fanaticism: The *Inferno Tour (35 euros | bookings at florence-museum.com)* will take you along Florence's back streets to rather esoteric places like the Dante house and the Badia tower: creepy, *davvero!* Slightly less mystical, but no less enlightening: Photographer Davide will take you on **INSIDER TIP** *a photo tour* through the city's back streets to point out Florence's hidden treasures. He is a veritable well of tips and tricks on how best to capture them on smartphone, SLR camera or digicam *(45 euros | bookings at www. facebook.com/ aphotowalkinflorence)*, punctuated, naturalmente, by pit stops on order to sample local food and wine. We guarantee that after three hours, you will see the city differently! Dancing instructor Antonio is a renaissance man of a different kind: After a relaxing wine tasting, he will teach you how to *swing* like a jazz-era pro. *(65 euros | bookings at: www.airbnb.de/ experiences/38037)*. You don't speak Italian? No problem: Antonio speaks English – and Hand and Feet, if necessary!

## ENTERTAINMENT

Florentines love their small bars and clubs with just enough room for a band or a DJ. You will find them in the quarter San Nicolò, in the city centre and on Piazza Dalmazia – look for *Kitsch* or *Zoe Bar* or the legendary Jazz *Club Firenze* (U D3) in *Via Nuova de'Caccini 3*. Start the evening with an aperitivo in one of the beach bars along the Arno, or two or three. If you like it classy, go for dinner at the *Dolce Vita* (U A4) *(Piazza del Carmine 6r).* Free spirits can take a stroll through the student and artists quarter Oltrarno.

### HANGAR (U D4)

The cocktails are probably the most conventional aspect of this, well, rather unusual bar. Once you have got your head around the bright indigo walls featuring Kamasutra instructions, you can feast your eyes on the colourful interior with Iranian, Columbian, Italian and Feminist influences. From 9pm, things will get more vivacious with live music or a DJ on the tiny stage. *Tue–Sun 9pm–1am | Via dei Pepi 43*

### LE MURATE (U E4)

Literary café, exhibition area, pizzeria, book shop and a stage: Florence finally has a public space for contemporary culture and it is in a beautifully restored former women's prison. *Daily | Piazza Madonna della Neve | www.lemurate. comune.fi.it*

### PLAZ FLORENCE (U E4)

Full-time place with urban food, terrace and live music on weekends. *Daily | Via Pietrapiana 36–38r | www.plaz.eu*

## WHERE TO STAY

### CASA HOWARD (U B3)

This guest house promises hip hospitality with, amongst other things, a room with a play corner for guests with children or one with a terrace for dog owners. *13 rooms | Via della Scala 18 | tel. 06 69 92 45 55 | www.casahoward.com | Expensive*

### OSTELLO TASSO (0)

Is this a colonial inn, a train station or someone's living room? A little of everything, as it turns out. But what else would you expect when a bunch of artists open

The banks of the Arno attract both runners and flaneurs

The Monastery of San Francesco on the top of the hill of Fiesole

a hotel for creative minds and connoisseurs in the artists quarter of Oltrarno? You can relax on cinema seats and watch performance artists and musicians do what they do best. A double room is quite affordable for Florence and a single is worth it just for the ambiance. *13 single and double rooms | Via Villani 15 | tel. 05 50 60 20 87 | www.tassohostelflorence.com | Budget*

### VILLA SESTINI ☀ (0)

Cosy B&B in a private villa on the southern hills with fantastic views all over the city. *2 rooms, 3 apartments | Via di Vernalese 21 | Bagno a Ripoli | tel. 0 55 63 09 51 | www.villasestini.com | Budget*

## INFORMATION

(U B3) | *Piazza della Stazione 5 | tel. 0 55 21 22 45;* (U C3) | *Via Cavour 1r | tel. 0 55 29 08 32 | www.firenzeturismo.it*

## WHERE TO GO

### CERTALDO (150 B3) *(𝓜 H9)*

The town of Certaldo, 45 km southwest of Florence (pop. 1600) is said to be the birthplace of Giovanni Bocaccio, the famous 14th century enfant terrible, writer, poet and humanist. Generations of young ladies have giggled and blushed their way through his saucy novella collection "Decamerone", in which many a husband is being cuckolded by his wife and nuns take turns with the gardener. The venerable German bard Goethe frowned upon it, but free spirit Herrmann Hesse was a big fan. In the *Casa Bocaccio*, his longtime domicile where he died in 1375 and now a museum, you can still imagine what life in the renaissance must have been like. Do take the funicular to get there, it is a bit of a climb but the view is spectacular! *(April–Oct daily 9.30am–1.30pm and 2.30pm–7pm, Nov–March Wed–Mon 9.30am–1.30pm and 2.30–*

*4.30pm/ 6 euros | Via Giovanni Boccaccio 18).* Back in the lower town, stop for lunch in the *Osteria La Saletta (Closed Tue | Via Roma 4 | tel. 05 71 66 81 88 | www.ostria lasaletta.com | Moderate).* Do make sure not to skip dessert.

### FIESOLE (146 C5) (*ⁿ K7*)

The town (pop. 14,500), which lies on a scenic height on the hills of Florence, can be conveniently accessed with the bus line 7. The setting of Boccacio's "Decamerone", it was not always a suburb for well-to-do Florentines. Long before Florence came to power, the Etruscan settlement Faesulae flourished here. A steep hill from the central Piazza Mino da Fiesole leads up to the ✂ *San Francesco monastery* that dates back to 1399, which has a quaint *mission museum (daily 9am–noon and 3pm–5pm | admission free).* The monastery garden leads down to the *San Romolo Cathedral* which dates back to the 11th century. Behind the cathedral is one of the hidden treasures of Tuscany, the *Museo Bandini (Fri–Sun 10am–7pm, winter 10am–5pm | admission 10 euros | Via Giovanni Dupré 1)* full of sacred art and terracottas. The admission ticket can also be used for the *Archaeological Park (Wed–Mon 10am–7pm, winter 10am–5pm | Via Portigiani 1)* with its Roman theatre, thermal baths and temple. In front of the turnstile is the entrance to the *Caffè del Teatro Romano (summer daily 9am–7pm, longer during evening events)* where you can sit on the outside terrace and enjoy a cappuccino or a pasta against a lovely backdrop.

The centrally located, friendly *Villa Sorriso (7 rooms | Via Antonio Gramsci 21 | tel. 05 55 90 27 | Budget)* proves that in fine Fiesole, Tuscan hospitality need not be expensive. If you do not want to stay for the night: a walk across the ● *Via Vecchia Fiesolana* will take you back to Florence

in an hour, starting at the seminary. Between the stone walls, time seems to have stood still.

### IMPRUNETA (150 C2) (*ⁿ J8*)

In this town (pop. 15,000) 15 km/9 mi south of Florence everything seems to be made from terracotta – even the postboxes! The building master Filippo Brunelleschi came here to source the bricks used to build Florence's cathedral dome. Today you can peek over artists' shoulders as they turn and fire the clay, amongst them *Mario Mariani (Via Cappello 29),* who still works according to the traditional methods.

### MEDICI VILLAS ★

A country estate with a garden for pleasure? The Medicis liked the idea so much that they had various splendid estates built around Florence between the 15th and the 17th century – today World Heritage Sites. The favourite was the *Villa Medicea (Mon–Fri 8am–6pm, Sat 9am–noon | Viale Gaetano Pieraccini 17)* in Careggi (146 C5) (*ⁿ J7*) which is on the northern edge of Florence, on the road towards Monte Morello. Designed by star architect Michelozzi, it is here that Cosimo I and Lorenzo the Magnificent surrounded themselves with artists and philosophers.

At the *Villa La Petraia (daily 8.15am–4.30pm, March–Oct longer, closed 2nd/3rd Mon | free admission | Via di Petraia 40)* in Castello (146 C5) (*ⁿ J7*) about 6 km/3.7 mi in the direction of Sesto Fiorentino, you can view the magnificent garden in the Italian style.

17 km/10 mi west of Florence in *Poggio a Caiano* (146 A5) (*ⁿ H7*) is one of the most beautiful villas, the ● *Villa Medicea (core time daily 8.15am–4.30pm, March–Oct longer, closed 2nd/3rd Mon | free admission | Piazza de' Medici 14)* which

was commissioned by Lorenzo I in 1480. White and symmetrical with a curved side staircase and wide terraces, it was the model for later Renaissance villa architecture. Frescoes by Andrea del Sarto, Filippo Lippi and Jacopo da Pontormo decorate the villa's rooms.

## MONTELUPO FIORENTINO
(150 B1) (*ஹ H8*)

The small town of Montelupo (pop 13,700) 30 km west of Florence is the mecca of the ceramic arts. Here, you can take the first steps on your way to become a master potter. You can take one- to five-day courses at the *Scuola Ceramica (Viale Antonio Gramsci 10 | tel. 05 71 54 11 11 | www.scuolaceramica.com)*. Slightly less ambitious connoisseurs visit the *Ceramics Museum (Tue–Sun 10am–7pm, Wed/Thu also 9pm–11.30pm | 5 euros | Piazza Vittorio Veneto 10 | www.museomontelupo.it)* or take home a piece of pottery from the *Bitossi* Ceramics factory shop featuring remainders of the current production *(Via Castelucci 10)*.

## SAN CASCIANO IN VAL DI PESA
(150 C2) (*ஹ J8–9*)

Do keep your eyes on the road – this is Tuscany at its most scenic and the spectacular view may make you forget that you are driving. INSIDER TIP *Take a Vespa* to scoot around the vineyards and olive groves and if you visit *San Casciano in Val di Pesa*, 20 km south of Florence, make sure to take the country road via Tavarnuzze and Sant'Andrea. Or potter along the panoramic Etruscan trade road to Panzano via Mercatale. Along the way you will find many an old vineyard that has left its mark on Tuscan oenological history.

Another scenic beauty inot to be missed is the road from San Casciano via San Pancrazio to Tavarnelle in Val di Pesa.

Take a break in the little bar in *Santa Cristina* in Salivolpe to sample the truly divine sheeps' milk cheese from the local *Fattoria Corzano e Paterno. (Via Paterno 10 | tel. 05 58 24 81 79 | www.corzanoepaterno.com)*. The Swiss owners also rent out five comfortable apartments and three holiday homes. (*Moderate–Expensive*).

## VALDARNO (151 E–F 2–4) (*ஹ L8–10*)

A local saying warns the inhabitants of the fertile Arno valley, between Florence and Arezzo, that "every now and again the Arno returns home". When it rains, the river swells with water from the mountains and turns into a raging torrent. Etruscans and Romans heeded the warning and built their settlements and roads in the hills.

In the Middle Ages, Florence built its strategic outposts in the river's flood plains and this lead to the development of some thriving towns, like *Montevarchi* and *Figline,* but they had to endure a number of destructive floods. Today the cathedrals of the modern age, i.e. outlet shops, are found here. *The Mall (daily 10am–7pm | Via Europa 8 | www.themall.it)* in *Leccio* has almost all the big fashion names under one roof. Prada fans can score twice: next door in the *Via Europa 2–4 (daily 10am–7pm)* and 30 km/18.5 mi further south on the SS 69 past Montevarchi in *Levanella (Sun–Fri 10.30am–7.30pm, Sat 9.30am–19.30pm)*.

Sting fans can pick up a special souvenir from the farm shop INSIDER TIP *Tenuta Il Palagio* near Figline *(daily 8.30am–12.30pm and 3.30pm–7.30pm | Via Sant'Andrea in Campiglia 11 | www.palagioproducts.com)*: Apart from olive oil, honey and vegetables from his farm, the shop features a selection of wines made from Sting's own vineyard with names like, naturally, „When we Dance",

Worth a closer look: Details of the façade of Villa Medicea in Poggio a Caiano

„Message in a Bottle" or „Sister Moon". If you are lucky, you will run into the proprietor himself or his wife, Trudy Styler.

## VALLOMBROSA 🌿 (151 F1) *(𝄞 L8)*

In 1020 Giovanni Gualberto founded a hermitage 1000 m/3281 ft up in the shady valley 40 km/29 mi east of Florence. Eleven years later he founded the Vallombrosan Order and began construction of the abbey, today a fortress-like monastery. In the *monastery pharmacy* (daily 10am–noon and 3pm–5pm) you can purchase elixirs made by the monks. However the real star up here is the INSIDER TIP large old forest. It is the perfect place for a few days of quiet contemplation with the brothers of the Vallumbrosan Order. They also keep their huge collection of ancient books very quiet, but you can view it by appointment *(Mon–Sat 9am–1pm | www.monaci.org)*. The *apothecary's shop* at the monastery *(daily 10am–12pm and 3pm–5pm)* is also worth a visit: The cremes and elixirs were made according to ancient recipes. And

do try their home-distilled spirits! Still up for another walk in the woods? On the way there, in *Donnini*, is the *Fattoria Montalbano (Via Montalbano 12 | tel. 05 58 65 21 58 | www.montalbano.it | Budget–Moderate)* offering eight bright holiday apartments and a wide variety of activities.

# PISTOIA

*(145 F4) (𝄞 G–H6)* **Almost the entire inner city of the provincial capital of Pistoia (pop. 92,000) around the spacious Cathedral square and the beautiful market square Piazza Della Sala is a pedestrian zone. This makes strolling through the city pure bliss, especially since the small, historic shops have not been entirely displaced by the generic fashion chain stores. You can enjoy a peaceful sundowner in the Piazza del Duomo and watch the swallows fly overhead without being bothered by traffic noise.**

The cathedral's campanile has become Pistoia's main landmark

### SAN ZENO CATHEDRAL ★

The 10th century Cattedrale di San Zeno is one of Tuscany's oldest churches. The striking Romanesque structure features a wealth of artwork of different epochs, for example the baptismal font by the renaissance artist Giorgio Vasari and the baroque pulpit. The Saint James chapel contains the precious silver altar (1287–1456). Generations of silversmiths worked on the altar's 628 relief figures. *Mon–Sat 10am–12.30pm and 3–5.30pm, Sun 8–11.30am and 4–5.30pm | chapel 3.60 euros | Piazza del Duomo*

### MUSEO DEL RICAMO ★

When you look at the beautiful Casualguidi embroidery, an ancient technique originating in the region, you will recognize many of the designs from the Romanesque churches of the region. The embroidery of the 19th century features especially creative delicate flower designs and flowing, almost transparent phantasy creations. *Tue–Thu 10am–1pm, Fri/ Sat and 1st Sun of the month 10am–1pm and 3pm–6pm | free admission | Via Ripa del Sale 3*

### PISTOIA SOTTERRANEA AND OSPEDALE DEL CEPPO

You can walk much of INSIDER TIP *underground Pistoia* under the Ospedale del Ceppo and look at the oldest remains of the city and technical innovations of days gone by, such as an olive press and a millwheel. *(tours daily 10.30am, 11.30am, 2/3/4/5pm, April–Sept Sat/Sun also 6pm | 9 euros | Piazza Papa Giovanni XXIII 15 | www.irsapt.it)* The hospital *Ospedale del Ceppo* itself *(Via Matteotti 9)* was built in 1277, which makes it one of the oldest hospitals in Europe. It was in use until 2013. The English language tour through underground Pistoia ends in the historic rooms with the Anatomical Theatre and the Medical Academy room with a remarkable collection of surgical instruments, for example the "Pistoian knife". If going underground is not for you, have a walk around the front of the building to enjoy the loggia with Santi Buglionis world-famous glaze frieze from 1525 portraying the "seven works of merci", the city's pride and joy!

### TRATTORIA DELL'ABBONDANZA

The locals swear by the regional specialities like the vegetable soups and the *fritto misto* made from chicken and rabbit. *Closed Thu lunchtime and Wed | Via dell'Abbondanza 14 | tel. 05 73 36 80 37 | Moderate*

### OSTERIA LA BOTTE GAIA

The lovely terrace with a view of the cathedral is one good reason to come here; another reason is their unusual interpretation of Tuscan dishes. *Closed Mon| Via del Lastrone 17 | tel. 05 73 36 56 02 | www. labottegaia.it | Moderate–Expensive*

### I SALAIOLI

Breakfast, lunch and dinner made from local produce and a view of the most beautiful piazza in town! *Daily | Piazza della Sala 20–22 | tel. 0 573 20 02 25 | www.isalaioli.it | Moderate*

## SHOPPING

### LA DOLCE PEONIA ◎

Confectioner Emanulea Regi experiments with organic ingredients in her bakery – try her delicious corn and blueberry biscuits! *Viale Petrocchi 122*

## LEISURE & WELLNESS

If you like mid-century vintage, this is the place for you: The gentlemen get their beard coiffed at *Thy Barber Shop (Via Cavour 38 | tel. 0 57 33 25 76 | www. thyarber.thyculture.it)* while the ladies are pampered from head to toe, aperitif in hand, at *Thy Madame (Via Cavour 8 | tel. 05 73 99 42 46 | www.thymadame. thyculture.it),* where the interior is picture-perfect 1950s and the staff is dressed and styled to match!

## ENTERTAINMENT

The *Piazza della Sala* is the best place to enjoy a leisurely pre-dinner aperitivo. Try the *Hengover (Tue–Sun 5pm–2.30am |*

*Via Castel Cellesi 1a)* and start off the evening with an all-inclusive aperitif for 8 euros. Every weekend in *Posto Nero (Via Luigi Galvani 4 | postonero.org),* there is a session with the best DJs in town.

## WHERE TO STAY

### HOTEL PATRIA

Pretty three-star hotel; calm, moderatlely priced and centrally located. *27 rooms | Via Crispi 8/12 | tel. 05 73 35 88 00 | www. patriahotel.com | Budget*

### VILLA DE' FIORI

In this hotel, right outside the city gates, you get the feeling that you are visiting your favourite relatives. Good food and massages round off this feel-good experience. *11 rooms, 2 apartments | Via di Biginao e Castel Bovani 39 | tel. 05 73 45 03 51 | www.villadefiori.it | Expensive*

## INFORMATION

*Piazza Duomo 4 | tel. 0 573 21 62 2 | www. turismo.pistoia.it*

## WHERE TO GO

INSIDER **TIP** ► ABETONE
(145 D2) (*ɷ F5*)
This may be a real surprise to many: Tuscany has a substantial ski resort area in the Apennines. Some 1900 m / 6232 ft high, it covers four majestic valleys, with modern facilities and 50 km / 31 mi of well maintained ski slopes with varying levels of difficulty. During the summer hiking enthusiasts come here to hike in the mountains. Simple, comfortable accommodation can be found at the family hotel *Primula (16 rooms | Via Brennero 195 | tel. 0 573 60 1 08 | www.hotelprimula.com | Budget).*

A few kilometres south-east, in *Rivoreta*, you can try your hand at traditional Tuscan crafts: In the *Museo della Gente Dell' Apennino Pistoiese (March–July and Sept/Oct Sat/Sun 10.30am–12.30pm and 3.30pm–5.30pm, in Aug Tue–Sun 10.30am–12.30pm and 4pm–6pm, Nov/Dec Sat/Sun 3pm–5pm | Via degli Scoiattoli | www.ecomuseopt.it)* you can experience what life in the Apennine Mountains used to be like and have a go at basket and fabric weaving.

### INSIDER TIP FATTORIA LE CELLE ●
(146 A4) (⌀ H6)

The owner, Guiliano Gori, has been inviting high-profile artists here since 1982. The artists create their artworks on site and the landscaped garden (8 km / 5 mi east of Pistoia in Santomato) now has over 60 sculptures and installations. Free viewing during summer but only by appointment: *www.goricoll.it*

### MONTAGNA PISTOIESE
(145 E–F3) (⌀ G6)

Secluded lakes, wild mountain streams and fortified stone villages attract nature lovers in the vast beech and chestnut forests of the Pistoia Mountains. Hikers who love culture can also enjoy the themed routes that take you through the hidden evidence of the past. Information is distributed at various locations of the *Ecomuseo della Montagna Pistoiese (www.ecomuseopt.it)*.

Follow a lonely mountain path, the *Sentiero della Ghiacciaia*, to the "museum of ice", *Punto Didattico del Ghiaccio*, to find out about the world before refrigerators and enjoy some home-made *gelato* while you learn about the forerunners of our handy kitchen companions – "ice houses" or *ghiacciaie*. Refer to the museum's website for further information, hiking map and guided tours. Not for the faint of heart: Near San Marcello

Pistoiese, the ✲ INSIDER TIP *Ponte Sospeso delle Ferriere*, a 227 m long and only 80 cm wide suspension bridge runs high above the little river Lima. But don't worry, the bridge is over 100 years old and very safe! Accommodation is in the suitably rustic *Agriturismo Il Gufo (4 apartments | Via Porta Viti 34 | tel. 34 70 59 91 59 | www.gufotuscany.com | Budget–Moderate)* at *San Marcello Pistoiese,* ideal for day trips. If you prefer to lounge around, you can enjoy the stunning mountain scenery from the edge of the swimming pool.

### MONTECATINI TERME ★
(145 E4) (⌀ G7)

A mixture of minerals, enriched with essential elements and salts over the course of millions of years: this is the secret of the healing waters of Montecatini Terme. The Romans already came here to be cured of liver ailments and rheumatism; celebrities like Guiseppe Verdi, the Shah of Persia and Gary Cooper have sipped on its warm healing waters. At the end of the 18th century the Tuscan Duke Pietro Leopoldo I created the spa around the thermal springs. Amongst others, he built the classical *Terme Leopoldine* and the glamorous ● *Stabilimento Tettuccio* with its magnificent column porticos and water fountains with marble counters.

Apart from this, the image of the resort town (pop. 20,000) which lies a good 15 km / 9 mi west of Pistoia, is dominated by its art nouveau architecture. North-east of the spa, a red funicular takes you up to the protected Montecatini Alto. If you want to spoil yourself you will be in good hands in the *Grand Hotel & La Pace (130 rooms | Via della Toretta 1 | tel. 05 72 92 40 | www.grandhotellapace.it | Expensive)*, the oldest spa hotel in the town. The region around Montecatini is also a favourite destination for gourmets, especially because a ● INSIDER TIP master chocolatier

A veritable temple of wellness: The Terme Tettuccio in Montecatini

*(Slitti | Via Francesca Sud 1268 | www. slitti.it)* is at work in the neighbouring village *Monsummano Terme*. A bit further to the south-east, through the magnificent Tuscan landscape, is *Lamporecchio* and the ecologically-run wine and olive estate ⓥ *Balduccio (Via Greppiano 31 | www.balduccio.it)* where you can sample the local produce. (Appointments for tasting sessions at *www.merum.info*)

## PESCIA
### (145 D4) *(𝑚 F6–7)*
Just 25 km / 15.5 mi west of Pistoia is the little town (pop. 20,000) of Pescia, famous for its beautiful flowers. The colourful flowers are sold early in the morning at the *Mercato dei Fiori* at the train station. A river, the Pescia, divides the medieval centre of the town in two parts. On the western shore lies the older, secular part. Its centre is the long *Piazza Mazzini*.

A little further down on the other side of the river, the *Bottega Donnini (Via Fiorentina 30)* with its brightly shining metal wares is well worth a visit: For 60 years, master coppersmith Giuseppe Donnini has been making beautiful pots, kettles, goblets and trinkets from tin, brass and copper. The wonderfully situated wine estate *Marzalla (Via Collecchio 1| tel. 0572 49 07 51 | www.marzalla.it | Budget)* with its seven apartments, garden and restaurant is the ideal base to set out for tours into the Nievole valley and the surrounding mountains.

## SAN MINIATO ★ (149 E–F2) *(𝑚 G8)*
Trufflehunter Teddy knows his job: When the poodle manages to sniff out a truffle, he will get a treat – and so will the participants of the **INSIDER TIP** *truffle tour (all year round | Info and appointments at truffleintuscany.it)*. "The town of the white truffles" (pop. 28,000) 40 km / 24 mi boasts the largest truffle ever found anywhere. That was back in 1954. Do enjoy a meal in the award-winning *Antico Ristoro Le Colombaie (Closed Mon and for lunchtime except Sun | Via Giuseppe Montanelli | tel. 0571 48 42 20 | www. lecolombaie.eu | Moderate)*.

"Feast of Herod", part of Filippo Lippi's fresco cycle in Santo Stefano Cathedral

## VINCI (145 F5–6) (🗺 G–H7)

This town (pop. 14,500) between Pistoia and Empoli is dominated by Leonardo da Vinci, who was born here in 1452. Two museums are dedicated to him. The more interesting one is the *Museo Leonardiano (daily 9.30am–6pm, summer until 7pm | admission 7 euros | Piazza dei Conti Guidi 2 | www.museoleonardiano.it)*. Here they do not concentrate on Leonardo the artist, but on the scientist and inventor. A footpath leads 3 km / 1.8 mile north to his *birthplace* in the town district of *Anchiano, (daily 10am–5pm, summer until 7pm | 2 euros)*. The path through the olive groves, forests and vineyards is very attractive.

# PRATO

(146 B4–5) (🗺 H–J7) **What with all the Karaoke bars, restaurant names such as "Orchid" and a marzipan Zen master in the window of the Patisserie Cualu, you might think you are in China, not in Italy.** And you would not be far wrong: Prato's

large Asian population has came here with the fabric industry, whose origins date back to the 14th century. Most of the prestigious labels are manufactured by Chinese tailors and seamstresses. And Prato's proud inhabitants (190,000 inhabitants hailing from over 100 nations) celerate everyday multiculturalism. For this is a trendy town: Its luscious palazzi, churches and parks are teeming with members of he avantgarde, and the romantic, medieval setting is home to experimental youth centres as well as modern art exhibitions.

## SIGHTSEEING

### CASTELLO DELL'IMPERATORE 🎏

The massive castle was built for Emperor Frederick II but he did not live to see the castle's completion. So there it stands: massive, imposing but great for a view of the city from the top. In the summer, there is an open air cinema in the castle. *April–Oct Mon and Wed–Fri 4pm–7pm, Sat/Sun 10am–1pm and 4pm–7pm, Nov–*

March Fri 10am–1pm, Sat/Sun 10.30am–1pm and 2pm–4pm | free admission | Piazza Santa Maria delle Carceri

## CENTRO PER L'ARTE CONTEMPORANEA LUIGI PECCI

This centre for contemporary art, which is situated 2 km / 1.2 mi south of the city centre, is also the starting point for organised tours, for example, to Henry Moore's marble sculpture on the Piazza San Marco. During the summer it is often open for concerts. Tue/Wed noon–8pm, Thu–Sun noon–midnight | 10 euros | Viale della Repubblica 277 | www.centropecci.it

## CHINATOWN

From Piazza San Domenico, walk along Via Vincenzo, then turn right into Via Luigi Borgioli. The restaurant Ravioli Liu at the next crossing is very popular with the locals. Turn right for the hipster haunt Caffetteria Utopia, a fusion of the European and the Oriental. On the way, have a look at the oddments in the windows of the Queensshop and enjoy the Piazza dell'Immaginario, an art installment that used the wood of the trees lost in the storm of 2015.

## SANTO STEFANO CATHEDRAL ★

Here the external pulpit on the corner immediately draws your attention. The Sacro Cingolo, a gold threaded wool belt said to work miracles, is displayed here several times a year. The green and white striped marble façade was added to the cathedral in 1386. In the impressive interior Filippo Lippi, a son of the city, painted two series of frescoes on the walls of the main choir chancel. Daily 7.30am–7pm (choir chancel Mon–Sat 10am–5pm, Sun 3pm–5pm) | 3 euros | Piazza del Duomo

## INSIDER TIP MUSEO DEL TESSUTO ●

Underneath the vaults of a former textile factory, the history of Prato's textile industry is documented with machines, production techniques and priceless fabrics from bygone centuries. Special displays complement the current collection. Tue–Fri 10am–3pm, Sat 10am–7pm, Sun 3pm–7pm | 8 euros | Via Puccetti 3 | www.museodeltessuto.it

## FOOD & DRINK

### ENOTECA BARNI

This restaurant has two faces: at lunchtime it is a cantina for business people and at night it becomes an elegant restaurant. Closed Mon evening, Tue evening, Sat lunchtime and Sun | Via Ferrucci 22 | tel. 05 74 60 78 45 | Moderate–Expensive

### LA LIMONAIA

In a former green house, chef Claudio Vicenzo experiments with Tuscan recipes and serves his creations on the outside terrace on summer evenings. Closed Mon and luchtime in the summer; in the winter Sun evenings, Mon–Wed and lunchtime except Sundays | Via Firenze 83 | tel. 05 74 59 25 15 | www.ristorantelalimonaia.it | Moderate–Expensive

## SHOPPING

### ATIPICO

The wine, the grain, the cantuccini biscuits, the cheese and the mortadella – everything in this shop has been made or grown in the region of Prato. Here, you can also buy ⊕ INSIDER TIP Wally perfums and beauty products, natural cosmetics made according to traditional recipes. If you would like to try before you buy, visit the Casotto Atipico in the Giardino Buonamici above Piazza Buonamici. Via Bettino Ricasoli 13

### OPIFICIO JM

This spacious concept store is showcase of local design, art, culture and lifestyle. Drinks and specialities in the Italia-Bar are "made in Tuscany". *Shop Tue, Wed and Fri 11.30am–7pm, Thu 2pm–10pm, restaurant closed Sun/Mon and Sat lunchtime | Piazza San Marco 39 | www.opificiojm.it*

## ENTERTAINMENT

### EX FABRICA

A bunch of youngsters have created a lush urbane garden in this old factory building, which is now a event venue for poetry readings, art exhibits and concerts. Ex Fabrica and Botanic Bar open at 6 pm. *Via Ferdinando Targetti 8–10 | www.ex-fabrica.it*

## WHERE TO STAY

### ALBERGO GIARDINO

Centrally located, clean rooms, private garage: all good reasons to choose this friendly city hotel. *28 rooms | Via Magnolfi 2–6 | tel. 05 74 60 65 88 | www.giardino hotel.com | Budget*

### VILLA RUCELLAI

Unpretentious rooms with a lot of character await you in this Renaissance villa 4 km/2.5 mi outside the city gates. *11 rooms | Via di Canneto 16 | tel. 05 74 46 03 92 | www.villarucellai.com | Budget*

## INFORMATION

*Piazza Buonamici 7 | tel. 0 57 42 41 12 | www.pratoturismo.it*

## WHERE TO GO

### MUGELLO

*(146–147 C–D 2–4) (ฌ J–L 5–6)*
Riding, cycling or rowing? There are many exciting ways for outdoor enthusiasts to explore the forests, villages and hermitages od the Mugello valley. Excellent information material is available at the tourism office *(Via Togliatti 45 | tel. 0 55 84 52 71 85 | www.mugellotoscana.it)* in *Borgo San Lorenzo*.
Those coming from Prato via the A 1 will find the exit to Barberino di Mugello and the *Barberino Designer Outlet Village (Via Meucci | www.outlet-village.it/barberino)*, where all the international fashion brands are represented. From there it is a stone's throw to the *Lago di Bilancino* reservoir popular with windsurfers, sailors and sunbathers. Two establishments

# LOW BUDGET

In Tuscany there are a lot of centrally located Christian guest houses that are a far cry from being monastic but you do have to book well in advance. One example is the *Istituto Gould (39 rooms | Via de' Serragli 49 | tel. 0 55 21 25 76 | www.istitutogould.it)* in Florence, where you can get an en suite double room from 50 euros.

You can fill up your water bottle for free at ⊗ several points around Florence – there is even one at the Palazzo Vecchio. Do your bit to reducing the amount of plastic waste.

The textile town Prato is a bargain hunter's paradise where you can find (almost) everything in the factory at half price: cashmere jumpers, underwear, leather goods... For a list of addresses click on the "Where to Shop" section at *www.pratoturismo.it*

rent out umbrellas and also provide bar and restaurant facilities.

One of the most beautiful villas in Tuscany, *Villa Le Maschere (65 rooms | Via Nazionale 75 | tel. 055 84 74 32 | www.villale maschere.it | Expensive)* in *Barberino* on the road to the Futa Pass is where you can enjoy all the amenities of a luxury hotel. At *Agriturismo Corzano (3 rooms and 3 apartments | Via Bolognese 26c | tel. 0 55 84 14 03 | www.agriturismo corzano.com | Budget–Expensive)* in Barberino everything revolves around beer and saffron. The family shows you around (by appointment).

On your way there you will pass the *Autodromo del Mugello (www.mugellocircuit. it)* racing circuit where motorcycle and Formula-1 events are regularly held. In Scarperia (pop. 7,800) you should not miss a visit at the knife museum *Museo dei Ferri Taglienti (June–Sept Wed–Sun 10am–1pm and 3pm–7pm, Oct–May Wed– Fri 10am–1pm, Sat/Sun 10am–1pm and 2.30pm–6pm | 5 euros | Piazza dei Vicari | www.museoferritaglientiscarperia.it)*.

Cut-rate: Take home some nice knives from Scarperia

You can buy cutting implements in all price and quality ranges at *Coltellerie Berti (Via Roma 43 | www.coltellerieberti. it)*. Agriturismo Sanvitale (8 rooms | Via Campagna 20 | tel. 05 58 40 11 58 | www. agriturismosanvitale.it | Budget)* 5 km / 3 mi to the east in *Luco di Mugello* offers simple accomodation. An ideal place to get a feel for the people, the food and the way of life of the Tuscan people.

As a contrast to this there is the **INSIDER TIP** nature reserve around the 1000 year old *Badia di Moscheta* 17 km / 10.5 mi north on the road to Firenzuola. Visitors come for the delicious Tuscan steak dish *bistecca fiorentina* served in the restaurant *Badia di Moscheta (Closed Mon/Tue | Via di Moscheta 898 | tel. 05 58 14 43 05 | Budget–Moderate)* opposite.

Vicchio (pop. 8000) in the southeast of the Mugello region is the birthplace of Giotto and Beato Angelico. What better place to get your creative juices flowing than visiting the house that Giotto was born in? Enjoy the multimedia exhibition about the artist's life and work and finish off with a painting class *(Sun 10am–1pm and 3–7pm, in the summer also Sat 3–7pm | with painting class 5 euros | appointments at 05 58 43 92 25 or ufficio. cultura@comune.vicchio.fi.it)*. Sample the local delicacies – chestnut products, sheep's cheese and tortelli with potato filling – in the cooperative shop ⊘ Il Forteto *(Closed Mon/Thu | www.forteto. it)* 5 km / 3 mi outside of Vicchio in the direction of Pontassieve.

# AREZZO, SIENA & CHIANTI

Red wine, saffron, Tuscan tobacco – there is a certain golden, dry and slightly tangy aroma to the southeast of Tuscany, of sun-dried fields and the herbs of the macchia. This is a landscape of wineyards and ancient forests, with two provincial capitals that are virtual treasure troves of art and history.

## AREZZO

(152 C4) ( N10) As soon as you enter Arezzo's sloping Piazza Grande, you will realize that this town is a bit... different. But this is what makes it perfect for artists, collectors and hunter-gatherers of the old and the exceptional. Rumour has it that up to one ton of gold per month

**WHERE TO START?**
It is not easy to find a parking space. Your best bet is to try the Via Pietri 27. An escalator takes you up to the **cathedral** and you'll also reach the Basilica San Francesco with the famous painting cycle in no time. A more relaxing option is to travel there by train – it is only a ten minute walk from the train station. From here you can go via the boulevard Corso Italia, with its elegant shops and little alleys, to the impressive Santa Maria della Pieve church and the centre of Arezzo, the Piazza Grande.

# Castles, churches, cloisters and many curves: the Middle Ages dominate between Casentino and the Orcia valley

passes through the capable hands of the local goldsmiths. The regional pottery with its delicate designs has been famous for millennia: Arezzo (pop. 100,000) was founded by the Etruscans and is therefore one of the oldest cities in Italy.

Take a stroll through the medieval old town at the foot of the nicely refurbished Medici fortress among sumptuous palazzi, shops and ancient relics and enjoy the panoramic views from the high plateau and marvel how it could be that this beautiful town has been largely overlooked by tourism. Do take advantage of the great deals for multiple tickets that offer entry into several museums.

## SIGHTSEEING

### CASA VASARI

This magnificent house is one of the few preserved artist homes of the Renaissance: built and occupied by painter and architect Giorgio Vasari (1511–1574). He is responsible for the Uffizi

The heart of Arezzo and – at the start of the month – its market square: the medieval Piazza Grande

Gallery in Florence and his artist biographies helped create standard works of art history. *Mon and Wed–Sat 8.30am–7.30pm, Sun 8.30am–1.30pm | 4 euros | Via XX Settembre 55*

### SANTI PIETRO E DONATO CATHEDRAL

One remarkable feature of this 13th century Gothic building next to the city park, the Passeggio del Prato, are the stained glass windows by Guillaume de Marcillat (16th century) but it also has another great art treasure, a small fresco of Mary Magdalene by Piero della Francesca in the left aisle. *Daily 7am–12.30pm and 3pm–6.30pm | Piazza del Duomo*

### MUSEO NAZIONALE D'ARTE MEDIEVALE E MODERNA

Do try not to stumble as you walk though this magnificent collection of medieval art: The 8th century sandstone sculptures, to be sure, are quite forgiving but the countless delicate and beautifully and artfully decorated renaissance vases and dishes are irreplaceable. *Tue 9am–1.30pm and 3pm–7.30pm, Thu 9am–1.30pm, Sat / Sun 3pm–7.30pm | free admission | Via San Lorentino 8*

### PIAZZA GRANDE ⭐

Does this asymetric, slightly sloping square seem familiar? You may well recognise it from the film set of Roberto Begnini's "La vita è bella" (Life is Beautiful). This square, which was designed as a market place, has been used as backdrop venue for events like the medieval knight's tournament, Giostra del Saracino, which was first held here in 1593. For a box seat from which to watch the hustle and bustle, find yourself a café table under the beautiful Loggia del Vasari (1537) or on the steps of the courthouse and the elegant Palazzo Fraternità dei Laici on the western side. The narrow town houses date back to the Middle Ages.

### SAN FRANCESCO

Behind the unadorned façade of this Gothic basilica is a major work from the early Renaissance: A ten piece ⭐ fresco by Piero della Francesca, the "Legend of the Holy Cross". After a lengthy restoration it is now quite luminous and back to its

reservation: summer Mon–Fri 9am–7pm, Sat 9am–6pm, Sun 1–6pm, winter Mon–Fri 9am–6pm, Sat 9am–5.30pm, Sun 1–5.30pm | tel. 05 75 35 27 27 or www.pierodellafrancesca-ticketoffice.it | Tickets collected from the tourism office next door | 8 euros | Piazza San Francesco 1

### SANTA MARIA DELLA PIEVE

Its lovely choir apse faces the Piazza Grande and its front, with its impressive combination of columns and arches from the 12th century, makes it one of the most beautiful Romanesque monuments in Tuscany. The bell tower is known locally as the "tower with a hundred holes" because of its 40 Romanesque twin windows. *Daily 8am–noon and 3.30pm–7pm | Corso Italia 7*

former glory. The artist worked for more than a decade on the 3230 ft² narrative, bringing to life the history of the Holy Land and setting it in his own Tuscany. Arezzo becomes Jerusalem and the Queen of Sheba becomes a Renaissance noblewoman. *Admission only with advance*

## FOOD & DRINK

### ANTICA OSTERIA L'AGANIA

Family-owned restaurant serving classic Tuscan dishes and seasonal specialities.

---

**MARCO POLO HIGHLIGHTS**

*Closed Mon | Via Mazzini 10 | tel. 05 75 29 53 81 | www.agania.com | Moderate*

### BIOLENTO ❀

The interior is a cheerful riot of colours and eclectic styles. Everything on the menu including the beer has been organically grown and produced and freshly prepared. *Mon–Wed closed, Thu–Sun noon–14.30pm and 6.30pm till late | Piazza San Michele 15 | tel. 05 75 178 85 09 | Budget–Moderate*

### CAFÉ PARIS

International cuisine seasoned with a certain je ne sais quoi, including hearty snacks and sandwiches. A good place if you like surprises: Be prepared to stumble into a karaoke or speed dating party. *Daily | Via Madonna del Prato 81 | tel. 05 75 29 40 03 | Budget–Moderate*

## SHOPPING

### DISCHI

Vinyl fans: this place is well stocked with classics of all eras from classic Italian rock to Indie pop. *Corso Italia 89*

### MERCATO DELL'ANTIQUARIATO

Every first weekend of the month the Piazza Grande is transformed into the biggest antiques shop in Italy.

## ENTERTAINMENT

### URBAN CAFÉ

The trendiest of the evening bars with live music on the weekends. *Mon closed | Via Giuseppe Pietri 41b*

## WHERE TO STAY

### BED & BREAKFAST ANTICHE MURA

The old town house in the city centre may look a little crooked, but the Lanchi family has transformed this flawed gem into a sparkling diamond. The rooms are named after female icons: Marilyn Monroe, Holly Golightly, Emma Bovary. *6 rooms | Piaggia di Murello 35 | tel. 05 7 52 04 10 | www.antichemura.info | Budget*

### GRAZIELLA PATIO HOTEL

Bruce Chatwin's travel stories inspired the creation of this peaceful city hotel in an old city palace. How about picking up a book to see if you can find the chapter that inspired the creation of your room? *10 rooms | Via Cavour 23 | tel. 05 75 40 19 62 | www.hotelpatio.it | Expensive*

## INFORMATION

*Piazza della Libertà 2 | tel. 05 75 40 19 45 | www.benvenutiadarezzo.it*

## WHERE TO GO

### ANGHIARI (153 D4) (𝖔 O9)

Enter the mountain through a passage near the parking area and emerge in a medieval labyrinth of steep, narrow alleys and dark archaded passages. The beautiful old centre of Anghiari (pop. 5800) has a few treasures to offer, for example shops that feature traditional Tuscan crafts. Busatti (Via Mazzini 14), a traditional weaving mill that specializes in exquisitely patterend, luxurious linen fabrics and creations is a place you definitely should not miss!

In case you want to stay longer, the rustic *Agriturismo Il Sasso (7 rooms, 2 apartments | district San Lorenzo 38 | tel. 05 75 78 70 78 | www.agriturismoilsasso.it | Budget)* 3 km / 1.8 mile out of town is a good choice. The owners will gladly organise cultural trips and other activities for you.

## CAMALDOLI (152 B1) (*M N7*)

This village founded in 1024 by Saint Romuald is characterised by magnificent scenery and wonderful tranquillity. The Camaldolese monastery *(Monastero)* and hermitage *(Eremo)* 45 km / 28 mi to the north is a destination for trips as well as a retreat for people who are searching for contemplation. First there is the massive monastery with its beautiful cloister as well as the monastery pharmacy.

In the Hermitage, you can visit the cell of the order's founder, the church and the chapter hall (by appointment only, tel. 05 75 55 60 21). Opening hours of the monastery daily 9am–1pm and 2.30pm–7pm, in the summer –7.30pm, hermitage 9am–noon and 3pm–5pm, in summer 9am–noon and 3pm–6pm, closed on Sundays during mass. Information about classes and accommodation: *tel. 05 75 55 60 13 | foresteria@camaldoli.it | www.camaldoli.it.*

## CASENTINO (152 B–C 1–2) (*M M–O 6–8*)

The secluded valley in the north of Arezzo, with the Pratomagno in the west and the Alpe di Catenaia in the east, is a world of its own. During the Middle Ages the massive mountain forests were retreats for monks and later for rich patricians who built their summer residences here. In 1990 a large area of the countryside, 135 square miles, was declared a national park and nowadays there are even wolves once again roaming amongst the trees. You can explore the 600 km / 373 mi long network of paths on foot, horse or bicycle. Information and maps are available in the visitor centre of the *Parco Nazionale delle Foreste Casentinesi,* e.g. in *Pratovechio (Via Brocchi 7 | tel. 0 57 55 03 01 | www.parcoforestecasenti nesi.com).*

The administrative centre is the *Bibbiena* (pop. 12,500) with its beautiful old town. The winding SP 208 takes you in an

Then a hideout for monks, now a refuge for wolves: Casentino National Park

easterly direction up the ● ☀ *Abbazia La Verna (www.santuariolaverna.org)* 1128 m / 3700 ft. The monastery is situated on a precipice in the midst of beech and spruce trees and was founded by Saint Francis of Assisi. It is here where his stigmata manifested itself in 1224. The

Narrow alleyways and steep, cobbled steps characterise Cortona

abbey's grey stone exterior may appear rather forbidding at first sight but its interior, is a lively labyrinth of chapels, churches and monk cells. There is also a cave where St Francis used to retreat to for his prayers. On www.diqui passofrancesco.it you'll find information on the **INSIDER TIP** pilgrim's way on his trail. You need not be a pilgrim to stay in the very affordable *sanctuary (Chiusi della Verna | tel. 05 75 53 42 10 | www.santuariolaverna. org | keyword accoglienza | Budget).*

## CORTONA ★ ●
### (152–153 C–D6) (🕮 O12)

Churches, medieval monasteries and stately palaces are huddled together between weathered stone walls, steep alleyways and cobbled stairs leading up into picturesque little squares. The ancient Etruscan town (pop. 23,000) sloping up a hill 30 km / 18.5 mi to the south looks exactly like the Tuscany of your imagination. The same could be said about the elegant guest house *Il Falconiere (22 rooms | district San Martino 370 | tel. 05 75 61 26 79 | www. ilfalconiere.com | Expensive)*, where there is also a master chef in the kitchen *(daily, Expensive)*. Street cafés invite you in, shops offer culinary delights and craft work, and in the Museum for Archaeology and City History *MAEC (April–Oct daily 10am–7pm, Nov–March Tue–Sun 10am–5pm | 10 euros | Piazza Signorelli 9 | www. cortonamaec.org)* you can admire the curious collections of ancient artefacts. Afterwards its over to the 11th century cathedral and its ☀ viewing platform. If you are feeling inspired by all those magnificient vistas, why not create your very own souvenir to take home and enroll in a ceramic workshop with the artist Edi Magi in the nearby village of Castiglion Fiorentino? *(Information and reservations tel. 05 75 68 01 81 | www. edimagi.com).*

## LUCIGNANO (152 B6) (🕮 M12)

You can hardly find a more vivid medieval castle village on a hill. When walking through this village (pop. 3600, 30 km / 18.5 mi south-west, altitude 414 m / 1358 ft) you understand how a settlement can develop within a fortress. The village is dominated by the impressive 16th century church, *San Michele Arcangelo*. The *Palazzo Pretorio*, decorated with crests and coats of arms, behind the church to the left is almost

300 years older. Stepping through the southern city gate *Porta San Giusti* is a trip to the Middle Ages and back.

## POPPI (152 B2) *(𝄞 M–N8)*

The 12th century medieval castle of Count Guidi is seen as one of the best preserved monuments of Tuscany. It is situated 40 km / 25 mi north of Arezzo and dominates the village (pop. 6200) and surrounding area. At Ponte a Poppi you turn left over an old stone bridge and go up a forested hill. At the junction is the *Osteria del Tempo Perso (Via Roma 79)* where they serve the best *panini* in the area. Walking through the castle's courtyard *Castello del Conti Guidi di Poppi (variable opening hours, see website | 6 euros | www.buonconte.com),* decorated with coats of arms, a curved staircase takes you into the living rooms. The chapel is quite beautiful, it has 14th century frescoes and there is a library with valuable manuscripts. Take some time to stroll across the *Via Cavour* lined with arches, to the Romanesque abbey church *San Fedele*.

## SANSEPOLCRO (153 E3) *(𝄞 P9)*

See the fields of high (up to 2 m), leafy shrubs with their pink or yellow flowers? This is Kentucky tobacco! The Tiber valley, Valtiberia, is Italy's main tobacco growing region. The leaf grown here will be dried, fermented and then rolled into Italy's cult cigar, the "Stortignaccolo". Manufacturer Gabriele Zippilli first smoked the local tobacco while at university, caught the bug and went on the establish his own factory directly at the source. You can visit the factory in Sansepolco (by appointment from Monday to Friday) to learn about the making of this Italian treasure: Compagnia Toscana Sigari *(Via della Commenda 103 | tel. 05 75 73 67 52 | www.compagniatoscanasigari.it).*

Sansepolchro, 35 km / 22 mi east of Arezzo, is also the birthplace of medieval painter Piero della Francesca (see no. 2 in the chapter on adventure trips). Here, you can learn about the ancient art of lace making: The bronze "statue of the lacemaker" near the gigantic 16th century loggia tells the story. The Boninsegni family have converted the manor house on their estate into holiday accommodation *(La Conca | 15 rooms and apartments | district Paradiso 16 | tel. 05 75 73 33 01 | www.laconca.it | Budget)* with a relaxed and friendly atmosphere. In the *tourism office (Via Matteotti 8 | tel. 05 75 74 05 36 | www.valtiberinaintoscana.it)* you can get information about the various themed walks, such as the one that follows in the footsteps of Piero della Francesca or where you can sample local specialities.

## LOW BUDGET

The term *vino sfuso* means "on tap" and many wine estates and shops sell wine this way. Even Chianti Classico or Rosso di Montalcino can be bought for less than half the bottle price. You only need an empty 5 litre bottle which can then be refilled again. Warning: vino sfuso is not wine that travels well.

The 28 simply furnished rooms at the *Casa per Ferie Betania (Via Severini 50 | tel. 05 75 63 04 23 | casaperferiebetania.com)* outside the gates to Cortona are lacking in comfort for a longer stay yet a double room with bathroom costs only 50 euros. The spacious garden and splendid ☘ panoramic terrace are priceless.

### STIA (152 A1) (*M7*)

Nature lovers know this pretty little village (pop. 3000) 40 km / 25 mi north of Arezzo on the slopes of Monte Falterone because it is the source of the Arno, blacksmiths because their world championships take place here every two years and fashion lovers for its *panno di lana,* a brightly coloured Tuscan fabric. This village also impresses with its long *Piazza Tanucci* and colourful houses. There is also the hotel and restaurant *Albergo Falterona (23 rooms | Piazza Tanucci 85 | tel. 05 75 50 45 69 | www.albergofalterona.it | Budget)* serving regional cuisine and the showroom for the wool cooperative T.A.C.S. *(www.tacs.it),* which has their outlet in the *Via Sanarelli 49*.

# SIENA

**MAP ON PAGE 62**
(151 D6) (*K11*)

**Siena (pop. 54,000) is an Italian marvel. Set high in glorious hill terrain and protected by fortified walls, it has managed to retain its medieval character right into the modern age. Strict building regulations have ensured that nothing disturbs the harmony of the cityscape. Even cars and television aerials are banned from its centre.**

The city is at its best about a week before the famous horse race, the Palio *(www.ilpalio.org)*. The whole place is already buzzing with excitement and good-natured banter, while music bands are performing in the streets. The medieval streets and passages are decorated in the traditional colours of the 17 participating city wards, volunteers tend the public flower beds and the Piazza del Campo is slowly transformed into a sand track for the upcoming races. The horse races take place every year on 2 July and 16 August.

Ten of the 17 districts, or *contrade,* of Siena compete against each other. The horses race around the Piazza del Campo three times and the winning *contrada* carry the standard or the *palio*. The Palio may be a bit controversial nowadays, but it still is the town's heartbeat and a central aspect of its identity.

You can book a visit to the museum of the ward of the Eagle, the **INSIDER TIP** *Museo della Nobile Contrada dell'Aquila (short.travel/tos4)* in the Palazzo Agazzari-Nastasi near the Piazza del Campo via the club's website (in Italian only). But this medieval pearl is worth a visit any day of the year. Thanks to the efforts of the tourist board, the music halls and museums are open all year round, so you can always book a guided walking tour or perhaps participate in one of the frequent sports events. Before the city walls you will find the metered parking area *(www.siena parcheggi.com)* but the bus is a far better option as it goes to the Via di Città which in turn leads to the Piazza del Campo.

## SIGHTSEEING

**INSIDER TIP** COMPLESSO MUSEALE SANTA MARIA DELLA SCALA

Almost 1000 years ago the Museum for Archaeology was a place where pilgrims on their way to Rome stayed overnight under fresco-decorated vaults and later the sick, poor and orphans were cared for. Today it is home to museums for archaeology, contemporary art and children. *Mid-March–mid-Oct daily 10am–7pm, Thu 10am–10pm, mid-Oct–mid-March Mon, Wed, Fri 10am–5pm, Thu, Sat, Sun 10am–10pm | 9 euros | Piazza del Duomo 2 | www.santamariadellascala.com*

### SANTA MARIA CATHEDRAL

The lofty nave of the 12th century cathedral is a feast for the senses, a riot

Black and white, the colours of Siena, also decorate the Santa Maria Cathedral

of stripes and arches, patterns, colours and light effects. The paintings show figures from another world or perhaps from another dimension, for today we would struggle to recognize the demons and fertility symbols as part of our Christian canon. Among the many highlights are Nicola Pisano's marble chancel turbulent scenes supported by lions, the frescoes of the *Libreria Piccolomini* on the left and the 15th century baptismal font by Jacopo della Quercia in the *Battistero San Giovani* on the left side of the cathedral. Unfortunately, you can see the marble mosaic floor from mid-August until the end of October only *(3 Euros surcharge)*. To wit: The groundbreaking of the cathedral took place in 1196 and the construction was completed in 1348. The building was planned on an even grander scale than it appears today

originally, what is now the nave was meant to be the transept! But then, as so often, money ran out and the nave perimeter remained a rudimentary wall. But while the city may have lost half a cathedral, it gained a fantastic ⚜ panoramic terrace. For an even better view (for instance from the cupola into the interiour of the church), take the INSIDER TIP ▶ *Porta del Cielo* tour of the cathedral roof. *March–Oct Mon–Sat 10.30am–7pm, Sun 1.30pm–6pm, Nov–Feb Mon–Sat 10.30am–5.30pm, Sun 1.30pm–5.30pm | 13 euros, Nov–Feb except Christmas / New Year 8 euros | www.operaduomo.siena.it*

## PALAZZO PUBBLICO

The city's town hall and its crenellated 90 m / 295 ft high ⚜ *Torre del Mangia* are stone expressions of Sienese identity and self-confidence. The brick building,

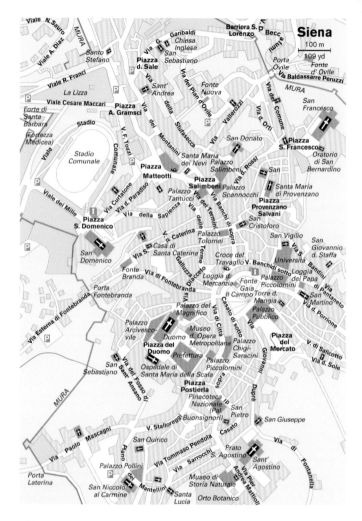

with Romanesque arches and Gothic cross vaults, houses some of the most important art treasures in Tuscany on its first floor: During the 14th century in the *Sala della Pace*, Ambrogio Lorenzetti painted a series of allegories of "good" and "bad" governments on the walls. In the *Sala del Mappamondo*, the map room, you will find one of Siena's oldest frescoes, a Maestà (Madonna with child, 1315) and the first large format landscape representation in European painting history, named after the commander Guidoriccio both by Simone Martini.

Every year in spring, the city opens the doors to the stanze segrete, the

**INSIDER TIP** "secret chambers", which normally serve as administration offices. From January, the exact date will be available on *www.comune.siena.it/Il-Turista/Turismo/News. Palazzo daily 10am–6pm, summer 10am–7pm, tower 10am–4pm, summer 10am–7pm | Palazzo 8 euros, tower 10 euros | Piazza del Campo 1*

### PIAZZA DEL CAMPO ★

The Piazza, sloping down to the *Palazzo Pubblico*, the town hall, owes its unique harmony and architectural integrity not only to its unusual shell shape, further accentuated by the white travertine stripes in the red brick paving that radiate out from the central water drain at the bottom. As early as 1300, an urban development scheme prescribed that all the windows of the surrounding Late Gothic "palazzi signorili" should have the same shape as the *Palazzo Pubblico* and that in contrast to earlier customs, the rooflines were to be in line with one another. Nowadays, the otherwise rather austere piazza is surrounded by busy restaurants and cafés with outdoor terraces.

The *Fonte Gaia*, a rectangular fountain created by Jacopo della Quercia in the 15th century, was extensively refurbished in the 19th century. It is a favorite meeting spot not only for the ubiquitous pigeons but also for locals and tourists, especially when the sun has finally wandered over the rooftops, leaving the square in soft evening twilight.

### PINACOTECA NAZIONALE DI SIENA

The patrician Buonsignori family bequeathed their beautiful city palace, with its elegant Renaissance courtyard fountain, to the province for use as a museum. It houses Siena's most important collection of paintings including works by Duccio di Buoninsegna and Simone Martini. *Tue–Sat 8.15am–7.15pm, Sun / Mon 9am–1pm | 4 euros | Via San Pietro 29 | pinacoteca nazionale.siena.it*

### CACIO E PERE

A firm favourite among the town's restaurants. The front of the establishment offers bar service, light lunches and an antipasti buffet while at the back local cuisine is served often accompanied by live music. *Closed Sun | Via dei Termini 70 | tel. 05 77 22 68 04 | Budget–Moderate*

### OSTERIA E ENOTECA SOTTO LE FONTI

Here you can enjoy traditional Sienese dishes like handmade *pici* noodles or *ribollita* soup. Directly opposite the Santa

The Torre de Mangia presides over Palazzo Publico and Palazzo del Campo

A Chianti Classico has to be made from 80 % Sangiovese grapes

Caterina car park. *Closed Sun | Via Esterna Fontebranda 118 | tel. 05 77 22 64 46 | www.sottolefonti.it | Budget–Moderate*

### TE KE VOI 🔖

Cold cuts, donuts or vegan platter – in this restaurant, all the food has been organically grown and is "km 0", meaning ultra local. The portions, which are fit for a king, are best enjoyed looking out through the gothic window onto the Piazza del Campo! *Daily | Vicolo San Pietro 4 | tel. 05 77 40 01 39 | Budget– Moderate*

## SHOPPING

### ANTICA PIZZICHERIA
### AL PALAZZO DELLA CHIGIANA
A couple of slices of air-dried ham suspended from the butcher shop's wooden ceiling, cheese and a fine glass of wine – gourmet heaven in the gruff but friendly heart of Siena. *Via di Città 93–95*

### TESSUTI FIORETTA BACCI
Scarves and jackets from the finest material, mostly handwoven. *Via San Pietro 7*

## SPORTS & ACTIVITIES

Dive further into the Tuscan cuisine by spending half a day at the *Scuola di Cucina di Lella* (tel. 05 74 66 09 | 100 euros / person | ww.scuoladicucinadilella.net) learning how to prepare regional dishes.

## ENTERTAINMENT

In the evening it is all about seeing and being seen around the *Croce del Travaglio*, where the boulevards *Via Bianchi di Sopra, Via Bianchi di Sotto* and *Via di Città* converge. A night bar for cool cats with a penchant for hot jazz: the *Tea Room (Daily 5pm–2.30am, closed on Mondays | Via Porta Giustizia 11).*

## WHERE TO STAY

### ANTICA RESIDENZA CICOGNA
Elisa Trefoloni turned her back on the teaching profession to transform her inherited family home into a comfortable bed & breakfast refuge. *7 rooms | Via delle Terme 76 | tel. 05 77 28 56 13 | www. anticaresidenzacicogna.it | Moderate*

## HOTEL MINERVA

This simple, well-equipped hotel is easy to reach by car, yet the centre is only a ten minute walk away. *56 rooms | Via Garibaldi 72 | tel. 05 77 28 44 74 | www.albergominerva.it | Budget*

## INSIDER TIP ▶ PALAZZETTO ROSSO

Do treat yourself to suite no. 7 on the palazzo's fourth floor: From the modern designer bed unter a nostalgic stucco ceiling, you will have a superb view over half the city! *9 rooms | Via dei Rossi 38–42 | tel. 05 77 23 61 97 | www.palazzettorosso.com | Expensive*

## INFORMATION

*Piazza del Duomo 1 | tel. 05 77 28 05 51 | www.terresiena.it*

## WHERE TO GO

### ABBAZIA DI MONTE OLIVETO MAGGIORE
(156 C2) (*Ø L12*)

Located 35 km / 21.5 mi to the south, a fortress-like gate and a cypress forest separate the abbey, built in 1313 on a windswept hill by the Olivetan order, from the outside world. The church has some beautifully engraved choir stalls with wood inlay; the massive cloister has 15th century frescoes of St Benedict painted by Luca Signorelli and Sodoma. In the *liquoreria* the friars sell herbal liqueurs. The monastery owns the simple *agriturismo Podere Le Piazze (6 rooms | Via delle Piazze 14 | tel. 33 84 95 91 47 | Budget)* in nearby *Chiusure di Asciano. Daily 9.15am–noon and 3.15pm–5pm, in summer until 6pm | www.monteolivetomaggiore.it*

### ABBAZIA DI SAN GALGANO
(155 F2) (*Ø J13*)

You might be excused to think that the massive monastery ruins 35 km / 22 mi southwest of Siena were built as a film set: Looking up from between the gothic arches, all you can see is a sky-blue cross where the roof should be. And indeed, the Cistercian monastery, built in 1224 and abandoned in the early 1500s, has served as the backdrop for Andrei Tarkovski's famous film "Nostalghia".

### ARCHEODROMO DI POGGIBONSI
(150 C4) (*Ø J10*)

40 km / 25 mi north of Siena, near the Medici fortress in Poggibonsi, archeologists have uncovered the ruins of a Carolinghian settlement and rebuilt it to the original specs right next to the site! Guided tours and reenactments of times gone by every Sunday afternoon. *April–Aug Sun 4pm–8pm, Sept–March 1pm–5pm | free admission | www.archeodromopoggibonsi.it*

### CHIANTI ★ ●
(151 D–E 2–5) (*Ø K–L 8–11*)

If you chose Tuscany as your dream destination because you have fallen in love with the quintessential picture of a country road winding its way through vineyards, holm oaks forests and cypress avenues to a remote farmyard, this is where you want to be. Here, in the Tuscan wine country between Siena and Florence, the *gallo nero*, the emblematic black rooster, crows over the local vineyards. Do make sure to visit at least one of the many vineyards of the region or, even better, book a tour at *(www.tuscan-wine-tours.com/super-chianti)* to avoid driving while over the alcohol limit. Cyclists will love the undulating hills, but if you prefer to take it easy, you can hire a Vespa or even a horse-driven chariot *(www.wagonrides intuscany.com)*. If you wish to stay longer, you can book idyllic rooms in one of the many refurbished farmhouses, for example *Il Colombaio (15 rooms | Via*

*Chiantigiana 29 | Tel. 05 77 74 04 44 | www. albergoilcolombaio.io.it | Budget)*. And it is not all olives and wine around here: Do try the saffron pasta, pesto or honey! You can learn everything about the "golden spice" and its history in the Chianti region at Agriturismo INSIDER TIP *Corte di Valle (tel. 0 55 85 39 39 | www.cortedivale.it)* on the SR 222 near Greve north of the Bolle city district – tasting included, naturally. Wine connoisseurs can sample local treasures 10 minutes away in the *Enoteca Ristorante Gallo Nero (Closed on Thu | Via Cesare Battisti 9 | Tel. 0 55 85 37 34 | www. pizzeriagallonero.it | Moderate)* on the Piazza Matteotti in the Greve city centre (pop. 11,000); further information a few steps away at the *tourist information (tel. 05 58 54 62 99)*. Epicureans and artists might like to stay in the B & B INSIDER TIP *Ancora del Chianti (8 rooms | Via Collegalle 12 | tel.0 55 85 40 44 | www.ancoradel chianti.it | Budget–Moderate)*, situated on a neighbouring hill in an ancient farmhouse. Here, you can choose between cookery, painting or languages courses. Radda in Chianti (pop. 1700) is a ⊗ „Centro Commerciale Naturale": Meat products, wine and even the colourful Pratesi shoes *(Via Chiasso dei Portici 9)* are all „made in Tuscany".

From Radda it is 10 km / 6 mi to the 1000 year old abbey with its cookery school, vineyard and gourmet restaurant INSIDER TIP *Badia a Coltibuono (guided tours of the cellar April–Oct daily 2.30, 3.30, 4.30 and 5.30pm , May–Sept also 6.30pm | 7 euros | 8 rooms, 5 apartments | tel. 05 77 74 48 32 | www.coltibuono. com | Expensive)* set in a magnificent forest. The SP 408 takes you back to Siena and along the way in Pievasciata is the *Parco Sculture del Chianti (April–Oct daily 10am–sunset, Nov–March by appointment only | 10 euros | tel. 05 77 35 71 51 | www.chiantisculpturepark.it)*, a private sculpture park that will pull you right back into the present with its contemporary art. Classical music and jazz concerts between July and September.

## MONTALCINO (156 C3) *(ᗪ L13)*

For a long time this fortified village (pop. 5000), 50 km / 30 mi south in an altitude of 570 m / 1870 ft above the Orcia valley was impregnable and it was only in 1560 that the Medici duke, Cosimo I, succeeded in occupying the last stronghold of the glorious Italian city republics. The tall and slender *Palazzo dei Priori*, on the Piazza del Popolo, is decorated with coats of arms and is a reminder of the village's great past. But the main reason people come here is to taste the award-winning red wine that has to be stored in oak barrels for four years before it can be called Brunello di Montalcino. In the *Enoteca della Fortezza (Piazzale Fortezza | www. enotecalafortezza.com)* you get expert advice. Good home cooking, a lovely atmosphere and good prices make the INSIDER TIP *Taverna del Grappolo Blu (daily | Scale di Via Moglio 1 | tel. 05 77 84 71 50 | www.grappoloblu.it | Moderate)* popular with locals and tourists.On the way between Montalcino and Castelnuovo dell'Abate lies the 12th century INSIDER TIP Romanesque *Benedictine abbey Sant'Antimo (daily 10am–5pm, April–Oct 10am–7pm | 6 euros)*. The rather severe basilica has a magical interior, illuminated by the sunlight that falls through its narrow windows.

## MONTEPULCIANO (157 E3) *(ᗪ N13)*

The walled vintners' town (pop. 15,000) on a hill 65 km / 40 mi south-east of Siena has always been very wealthy and could afford the best architects. During the 15th century Michelozzo built the *town hall* in the style of Florence's Palazzo Vecchio and during the 16th cen-

In early summer the abbey of Sant'Animo is surrounded by a sea of poppies

tury Antonio di Sangollo designed the *Palazzo Tarugi* and the *Madonna di San Biagio* church with its distinctive cupola. Besides the red wine Vino Nobile di Montepulciano, the contemporary music and theatre festival *Cantiere Internazionale dell'Arte (www.fondazione cantiere.it)* at the end of July / beginning of August, now also attracts a lot of visitors to the town. The *Caffè Poliziano (daily | Via Voltaia del Corso 27–29 | www. caffepoliziano.it)* is the most beautiful café in Tuscany, and *La Bottega del Nobile (Via di Gracciano nel Corso 95 | www.vino nobile.eu)* the most beautiful wine cellar in the town. Popular souvenirs are leather notebooks and bags by *Maledetti Toscani (Via Voltaia nel Corso 40 | www. maledettitoscani.com)*.

## MONTERIGGIONI (150 C5) *(M J11)*

On a hill 10 km / 6 mi north is this fortified, circular medieval village (pop. 9000). Its towers, erected in 1203, were described by Dante as looking like "giants guarding

the gates of hell". In the only hotel within the walls, the *Hotel Monteriggioni (12 rooms | Via 1 Maggio 4 | tel. 05 77 30 50 09 | www.hotelmonteriggioni.net | Expensive)*, transports one to another world.

## PIENZA (157 D3) *(M M13)*

After the mystical Middle Ages, man was once again allowed to be the focus and this meant that there were some new principles in urban design that reflected clarity and rationality. Ideas that came into play when Pope Pius II commissioned the Renaissance architect Bernardo Rossellino in 1460 to transform his home town into the "ideal city". First of all he designed an outdoor community square, the Piazza Pio II. Around it he arranged the bishop's palace (Palazzo Piccolomini), the city hall with its arches, and the spacious cathedral. He used an optical trick – the sides of the square make a trapezoid – giving the illusion of volume. An osteria that is a culinary must is the *Sette di Vino (Closed Wed | Piazza di*

*Spagna 1 | tel. 05 78 74 90 92 | Moderate)* serving delicious local specialities. In Camprena 6 km / 3.7 mi further north, is a rather special place to stay, the agriturismo INSIDER TIP *Sant'Anna in Camprena (20 rooms and 3 apartments | district Sant'Anna in Camprena | tel. 05 79 74 80 37 | www.camprena.it | Budget)*, a former monastery that was the location for the film "The English Patient".

**SAN GIMIGNANO ★ (150 B4) (*⊞ H10*)**

The higher, the more powerful: this town (pop. 8000, 45 km / 28 mi north-west) owes its landmarks to this medieval contest of vanity, this architectural epitome of one-upmanship: a whole town dominated by the towers on the palazzi of the rich and noble families: The almost 54 m / 177 ft high towers, of which 15 have been preserved, are the reason that millions of tourists come to this fortified town. As soon as the fuss is over at night, the medieval streets and cobbled squares belong to the locals again.

On the main square, the *Piazza della Cisterna* with its travertine fountain, is the hotel and restaurant *La Cisterna (48 rooms | tel. 05 77 94 03 28 | www.hotelcisterna.it | Moderate)* that has had a good reputation for many years and in the *Gelateria di Piazza (daily)* a master ice cream maker is at work. The Piazza Duomo is full of medieval gems that you should not miss: the *Santa Maria Assunta* (1148) church with its frescoes and its broad staircase, the *Loggia del Battistero* with the mural from the workshop of Domenico Ghilandaio (1476), the 12th century *Palazzo Vecchio del Podestà* with its large archway and the coat of arms bedecked *Palazzo del Popolo,* where the *city museum (April–Sept daily 10am–7pm, Oct–March 11am–5.30pm | 9 euros | www.sangimignanomusei.it)* is housed. It has the same opening hours as the *Torre Grossa* next door which has a panoramic view over the whole Elsa Valley.

Amongst the town's craftsmen, Franco Balducci stands out with his exquisite ceramic designs: INSIDER TIP *Ceramica Balducci (Piazza delle Erbe 5 | www.balducciceramica.com).* In the *Osteria del Carcere (Closed Wed | Via del Castello 13 | tel. 05 77 94 19 05 | Moderate)* you are served – typically Tuscan – soup as *primo* instead of pasta.

**VAL D'ORCIA ★ (156–157 C–D 3) (*⊞ M13–14*)**

The unique landscape south of Siena is known as the "land of wind and desert" or *le Crete Senesi* because of its characteristic clay soil which dries out during the summer. The sandy and barren landscape holds a magnetic fascination. In places the lunar landscape – which is interwoven with wheat fields, vineyards and olive groves – has hardly changed in centuries. Instead of new buildings, traffic and industrial sites, here one sees endless rolling hills, tall cypresses, isolated farmsteads, ancient monasteries and medieval mountain strongholds. Today the expansive valley between Buonconvento, Monte Amiata and Montepulciano is Parco Artistico, Naturale e Culturale della Val d'Orcia *(www.parcodellavaldorcia.com),* a nature and cultural park and Unesco world heritage site.

On public holidays and during local festivals, the region's peaceful silence is broken by the steam engine whistle of the nostalgic *Treno Natura (www.terresiena.it/it/trenonatura)* huffing and puffing through this lunar landscape.

The park headquarters are in the beautiful village of *San Quirico d'Orcia*. Along the way are some ancient thermal baths ideal for you to revive your body and mind. The hot sulphur springs of *Bagno Vignoni* are something special. The steaming, open baths from the Middle Ages may no longer be in use but the modern versions will certainly do the trick at the *Hotel Posta Marcucci (36 rooms | tel. 05 77 88 71 12 | www.hotelpostamarcucci.it | Moderate)*.

### VOLTERRA ★ (149 F5) (*G11*)

The picturesque town is known for three things: Tufa, alabaster and vampires. Yes, you heard correctly: After the immense success of Stephenie Meyer's Twilight Saga, her readers know that Volterra is the home of a ancient vampire clan. You can even take a vampire themed tour *(35 euros | www.newmoonofficialtour.com)*. The Etruscans built the town (pop 11,000) on top of a tufa hill. Velatri (Voterra's Etruscan name) was part of the Dodecapolis, a league of twelve settlements for mutual protection. Today, Volterra needs protection mainly from the elements, for the foundations of the town are slowly being undermined by wind and rain.

Coming from Siena, 50 km / 31 mi away, you enter the fortified old town through the *Porta Selci* at the Medici fortress. Just behind it is the *Museo Etrusco Guarnacci (daily 9am–7pm, winter 10am–4.30pm | 14 euros | Via Don Minzoni 15)*. The collection includes the thin bronze statuette *Ombra della Sera* (Evening Shadow) and also the symbol of Etruscan art, the sarcophagus depicting a married couple lying down. In the *Viale Gramsci 70* local cuisine is served in the friendly *Trattoria Ombra della Sera (Closed Mon | tel. 05 88 88 66 63 | Moderate)*.

From the Via Gramsci turn right to the *Roman Theatre*, which is still being used as a summer stage, and left along the Via Matteotti to the beautifully preserved *Piazza dei Priori*. Here you can see the oldest town hall in Tuscany, the *Palazzo Priori* (1208–54,) and the *Palazzo Pretorio*, also from the 13th century with a tower and loggia. To get to the 4th century *Arco*

It's all in the fingertips: Ceramic artist Franco Balducci

*Etrusco*, one of the few surviving Etruscan city gates, you need to cross the Piazza San Giovanni with the 12th century *Santa Maria Assunta* Cathedral and its octagonal baptistery.

The family-owned business **INSIDER TIP** ▸ *Rossi Alabastri (Piazza della Pescheria | www.rossialabastri.com)* has the best reputation among Volterra's alabaster workshops. The best place to recuperate after your vampire tour is in the large park of the hotel *Villa Nencini (32 rooms | Borgo Santo Stefano 55 | tel. 058 88 63 86 | www.villanencini.it | Budget)*.

# MAREMMA & COSTA DEGLI ETRUSCHI

If you want to travel through the Maremma in style, it should be on horseback. After all, the region boasts its very own breed of horse, the agile Maremmano. But if you find a bicycle saddle more reassuring, you are also in the right place; in fact, this is the place to be for all those who love wide open spaces. The wild, rugged landscape is full of surprises: primeval cattle, ancient Etruscan sites, modern music and culture, hot springs and the rocky Tyrrhenian coastline alternating with sandy beaches lined with pine avenues. The nightlife in the beachside resorts is more casual and relaxed than in the swanky beach resorts further north in the Versilia.

The 90 km long *Costa degli Etruschi (www.visitcostadeglietruschi.com)* between Livorno and Piombino with its sand and pebble beaches and rugged cliffs is a paradise for sunbathers and snorkelers alike. Family-friendly holiday resorts nestled between the pine forests offer a wide spectrum of activities for all ages, while the spirit of the ancient Etruscans pervades the hilly hinterland.

## GROSSETO

(158 B1) (*∅ J16*) In the pedestrian areas of the city centre, you can have a leisurely stroll along shady arcades and alleyways and enjoy the busy cafés, swanky bars and quirky taverns untroubled by traffic noise. Shopaholics find all the leading branches along the main

Photo: Maremma near Alberese

## No chance of boredom: Tuscany's tourist paradise between Monte Argentario and the Etruscan coast

streets as well as small, local artisans and specialty shops a little further afield: for instance, for leather goods, shoes, vinyl records or comic books.

The former episcopal seat (pop. 80,000) does not have many architectural monuments: Recurrent malaria epidemics kept the people away from the marshy swampland, which was first successfully drained around the time of World War 2. Nowadays, however, the region has become the Maremma's vegetable garden and you can buy fresh *frutta e verdura*

fresh from the field all along the country roads.

### SIGHTSEEING

#### FORTEZZA MEDICEA

You can walk around the centre on top of the broad walls of the hexagonal ramparts from the 16th century. During its construction, the old citadel *(Cassero Senese)* was integrated into the new town walls. Today it houses the tourist information. The moat around the city

A size smaller but in the Sienese style: The Duomo and Piazza Dante

wall was in use until 1835 when it was filled in and turned into parks and streets.

### MUSEO ARCHEOLOGICO
### E D'ARTE DELLA MAREMMA

In the city district of Marina di Grosseto, a young team of chefs serves delicious seafood right on the beach. Best book early – and do remember to take the mosquito repellent! *April / May Tue–Fri 9.30am–4pm, Sat / Sun 10am–1pm and 4–7pm, June–Sept Tue–Fri 10am–6pm, Sat / Sun 10am–1pm and 5–8pm, Oct–March Tue–Fri 9am–2pm, Sat / Sun 10am–1pm and 4–7pm | 5 euros | Piazza Baccarini 3 | maam.comune.grosseto.it*

### PIAZZA DANTE

In the 19th century the city gave its central square an historic renovation to polish up its prestige. The 14th century Romanesque-Gothic *cathedral* received a marble façade in the medieval Sienese style, the new town hall was built in the style of the Gothic Florentine palaces and the new provincial administration building was

modelled on Siena's town hall. The monument in the centre of the square is dedicated to the Duke of Lorraine, Leopold II.

## FOOD & DRINK

### LA BUCA DI SAN LORENZO

This restaurant, in the city wall, has for years been regarded as the best in the city. Host Claudio Musu never rests on his laurels and always comes up with new combinations. *Closed Sun / Mon | Viale Manetti 1 | tel. 0 56 42 51 42 | Expensive*

### ESSENZA ● ◉

Right by the parking area before the city walls, you can browse for books while enjoying your coffee, *gelato* or even a leisurely glass of wine, snack on *panini* or sample the vegan buffet if you are hungry. Everything is vegan, organic, home cooked and mostly local. On some evenings, there are movies, music or other cultural events. *Tue–Sat 7am–10.30pm, Sun / Mon 7am–8pm | Piazza Esperanto 7 | Tel. 0 56 41 93 02 81 | Budget–Moderate*

**FIUMARA BEACH**
In the city district of Marina di Grosseto, a young team of chefs serves delicious seafood right on the beach. Best book early – and do remember to take the mosquito repellent! *Daily | Fiumara district | tel. 0 56 43 40 40 | www.fiumara beach.it | Expensive*

## SHOPPING

**FARMER'S MARKET ⊗**
When the yellow flags from the Coldiretti farmers' association are flying, local farmers have gathered to sell fruit, vegetables and local specialties. *Wed and Sat 8am–1pm | Via Roccastrada 2*

**INSIDER TIP ▶ I VINI DI MAREMMA ●**
If you want to take a bit of Maremma home with you, pay a visit to the cooperative on the SS 332. You'll find local wines and culinary specialities from the farmers in the region. *Il Cristo district | Marina di Grosseto | www.ivinidi maremma.it*

## BEACH

Sunbathing, kitesurfing, paddling, sailing, walking: during the summer the coastal village of Marina di Grosseto becomes one large outdoor recreational park where you can choose between a public beach and a manicured lido *(bagno)*.

## ENTERTAINMENT

**INSIDER TIP ▶ COMIX CAFÉ**
The tree fountain on the piazza looks like something out of the Lord of the Rings. Small wonder, for it is right opposite the Comix Café, a quirky coffee bar with occasional live music and a shop for comics, fantasy and board games. Read your comic on the outside terrace with a cup of coffee, play a board game or just enjoy the running water. *Mon–Fri 7.30am–midnight, Sat 11am–midnight | Piazza San Michele 4 | www.comixcafe.it*

**PUB IRISH SOUL**
The pub, in the city's oldest house, stocks a wide range of good European beers so even in the middle of the Tuscan wine lands there are people who appreciate a beer! *Daily 6pm–2am | Piazza del Mercato 23*

## WHERE TO STAY

**AGRITURISMO SAN LUIGI**
In their authentic and family-friendly holiday home located 5 km / 3 mi from the coast between Grosseto and Castiglione, Susanna and Vanni have thought of everything you need to forget your worries. *2 rooms, 3 apartments | Cernaia district 700 | tel. 05 64 40 41 12 | www.podere cernaia.it | Budget–Moderate*

## INFORMATION

*Cassero Senese on the city wall | tel. 05 64 48 85 73;* otherwise: *Via Colombo 5 | www.turismogrosseto.it*

## WHERE TO GO

**CASTIGLIONE DELLA PESCAIA**
(155 D6) (*ロ G16*)
From the region's cleanest beach, you can see the island of Elba floating far away in the summer haze. Typical Mediterranean holiday atmosphere and an award-winning beach with crystal clear water are just two of the advantages of this village (pop. 7500) 20 km / 12,5 mi west. A thick line of pine trees shelters the mile-long sandy beach, colourful fishing boats bring in their fresh catch daily. The fresh fish is excellently prepared at *La Casa Rossa (Closed Mon in winter | Via Paolini 45 | tel. 05 64 93 35 71 | Moderate)*. Along the beach promenade one *bagno* is squeezed in next to the other and in the evening holidaymakers stroll along the promenade past bars, shops, restaurants and the popular ┃INSIDER TIP┃ *Gelateria Paradise (daily 10am–2am | Via Vittorio Veneto 13)*. The *Hotel Miramare (37 rooms | Via Vittorio Veneto 35 | tel. 05 64 93 35 24 | www.hotel miramare.info | Moderate)* is situated directly on the seaside.

**IL GIARDINO DEI TAROCCHI**
(159 E4) (*ロ L18*)
A fantasy sculpture garden with 22 colourful Tarot symbols that seem to grow out of the ground. The French artist Niki de Saint Phalle (1930–2002) had the garden created. For a visit you have to travel 60 km / 37 mi to the south and leave the four-lane coastal road Aurelia at the Pescia Fiorentina exit. *April–mid-Oct daily 2.30pm–7.30pm, Nov–March 1st Sat of the month 9am–1pm | 12 euros, free admission Nov–March | ilgiardino deitarocchi.it*

**IL GIARDINO DI DANIEL SPOERRI** ★
(156 C4) (*ロ L14*)
In his sculpture garden, on the northern slopes of Monte Amiata in Seggiano 65 km / 40 mi north-east of Grosseto, the Swiss sculptor Daniel Spoerri displays his own sculptures and those of his friends. Here one of Jean Tinguely's scrap machines rumbles into life at the press of a button, Jesús Soto's sound sculpture whistles in the wind on a small hill and visitors trip over bronze slippers cast by Spoerri himself. *Easter–Oct Tue–Sun, July–mid-Sept daily 11am–8pm, Nov–Easter by appointment only | 10 euros | tel. 05 64 95 08 05 | www.danielspoerri.org*

**MAREMMA**
(158 A–B 1–3) (*ロ H–J 16–17*)
Who invented the cowboys? Well, the Americans most certainly did not: Cowherds on horseback were known at least since the time of the Etruscans. The ● *butteri d'Alta Maremma* on their strong, agile horses are the last survivors of the dying breed of cowboys of the Maremma plains, looking after the large and primeval looking Maremmana cattle with their long, impressive horns. If you are a seasoned rider and would like to have a go yourself, you can spend a day with the

*butteri* in the ★ ◉ *Parco Regionale della Maremma*. But even beginners can explore the Maremma INSIDER TIP on horseback: book a tour at Cavallonatura *(Strada del Pingrossino | Tel. 32 89 78 40 18 | www.cavallomaremma.it)* near the coast at Marina di Grosseto.

If you prefer solid ground underfoot, you can take a walk around the stables, the *butteri* museum and the tavern or watch a rodeo in the summer. Find out all about it at *www.butteri-altamaremma.com* and – in Italian only – at *www.alberese.com*. Visitors must use the park entrances at Alberese or Talamone and strictly stick to the roads. In the park, tour guides will accompany you on a wide range of activities from night-time walks to ● INSIDER TIP canoe tours. Information about activities, accommodation, food etc. in *Centro Visite Alberese (summer daily 8am–8pm, winter 8.30am–1.30pm | Via Bersagliere 7–9 | Tel. 05 64 40 70 98 www.parcomaremma.it)* and online at *www.naturalmentetoscana.it* and *www.turismoinmaremma.it.* In the evening after an eventful day of hiking, paddling and horse or bike riding, relax at a jazz or traditional music concert. A great place for the environmentally conscious is the ◉ *Country Resort Le Due Ruote (17 rooms, 4 apartments | Strada Antica Dogana 44 | tel. 05 64 40 53 61 | www.agriturismole dueruote.it | Budget–Moderate)* in Alberese. Like the park itself, the restaurant *Da Remo (Closed on Wed | Strada Provinciale 59 | Tel. 05 64 40 50 14 | Moderate–Expensive)* has not changed in many decades, especially with regard to the quality of their fish recipes.

## MASSA MARITTIMA ★
(155 D3) (*ω G13–14*)

It is easy to lose your heart to this medieval mining town (pop. 9000) 50 km / 31 mi to the north: an aperitif at sunset on the Piazza Garibaldi, the view over the vast countryside to the sea from the ⚬ de-

The cowboys from Maremma: *Butteri* are shepherds on horseback from the Azienda Alberese

fence tower *Torre del Candeliere (summer Tue–Sun 10am–1pm and 3pm–6pm, winter 11am–1pm and 2.30pm–4.30pm | 3 euros)* on the Piazza Matteotti and a stroll through the alleyways of the Romanesque lower town up to the Gothic upper town Città Nuova are only some of the reasons. The fact that the town centre is so well preserved is because malaria forced its citizens to flee during the 15th century. The town lay, like a Sleeping Beauty, for four centuries before people began to return to it. The *Piazza Garibaldi* in the lower Città Vecchia is the centre and can be reached from the Piazzale Mazzini in the east. There, surrounded by travertine palaces and perched on a platform, is the beautiful cathedral, *San Cerbone,* with its wonderful 11th century Christian reliefs.

A few steps further in the *Taverna del Vecchio Borgo (Closed Sun evening and Mon | Via Parenti 12 | tel. 05 66 90 39 50 |*

*Moderate)* they serve typical game dishes. 10 km / 6 mi south of the city is *Tenuta del Fontino (23 rooms, 6 apartments | Accesa district | tel. 05 66 91 92 32 | www.tenutafontino.it | Moderate)*, a wine estate with swimming pool, forest lake and horseback riding, where the landlady hailing from South Tyrol will make you wonderfully welcome.

**MONTE AMIATA** ⊙ (157 D5) (*M15*)
On clear days, the characteristic cone shape of the extinct volcano (1738 m / 5702 ft) can be seen throughout Tuscany. It has been quiet for 180,000 years. Nevertheless, its remote, lushly forested slopes are a well-kept secret. For centuries, the population here has lived on its mineral resources but since the last cinnabar mine closed during the 1970s, the area has started to rely on sustainable, eco-tourism with plant and animal protection areas being set up, as well as a dense network of themed hiking trails, amongst them the INSIDER TIP chestnut trail, *Strada del Castagno.*
Free hiking maps are available in the

## LOW BUDGET

The Livorno Card (in Punto Informazioni | Via Alessandro Pieroni 18) is a great way to save money. For 3 euros per day (or 5 euros for three days) you can visit various museums in Livorno, use the city bus and get discounts at the aquarium and on boat trips.

A double room with private bathroom for 70 euros in Massa Marittima? The local Fransiscan monastery is allowed to rent out a section of the monastery as holiday accommodation: ● *Domus Bernardiniana (38 rooms | Via San Francesco 10 | tel. 05 66 90 26 41 | www.domusbernardiniana.it)*

The Piazza Garibaldi in Massa Marittima's Città Vecchia is seldom this empty

tourist office (Via Adua 21 | tel. 05 77 77 58 11 | www.terresiena.it) in the main village *Abbadia San Salvatore* (pop. 7000), 75 km / 46.5 mi east of Grosseto on the eastern flanks of the Monte Amiata.

There it is worth visiting the oldest Tuscan *abbey (daily 7am–7pm)* dating back to the year 750, with a crypt supported by 36 columns and the *mine museum Museo Minerario (mid-June– Oct daily, otherwise Mon–Fri 9.30am– 12.30pm and 3.30pm–6.30pm | 7 euros | Piazzale Rossaro 6 | guided tour by appointment via tel. 05 77 77 83 24 | www. museominerario.it),* where the history of cinnabar mining is documented. The hotel and restaurant *Fabbrini (35 rooms | Via Cavour 53 | tel. 05 77 77 99 11 | www. hotelfabbrini.com | Budget–Moderate)* in an old city villa, has simple, yet comfortable accommodation.

The most beautiful place (pop. 3000) on Monte Amiata is *Santa Fiora*, enter the village from the south and just after the bridge, on the Piazza Garibaldi, you will come across the oldest part of the village,

the *Castello,* with the remains of a castle, a clock tower and a Sforza family Renaissance palace. The Via Carolina leads you to *Al Barilotto (Closed Wed | Via Carolina 24 | tel. 05 64 97 70 89 | Moderate)* where you can order tasty local food, to the *borgo* district at the foot of the Castello. *Montecatino* lies just outside the city walls and is famous for the giant fish pond from the 15th century, the *Peschiera*, which collects water from the Fiora River.

## MONTE ARGENTARIO
(158 B–C 4–5) (*ฒ J18–19*)

Turquoise water, white sandy bays and rugged cliffs line the promontory 45 km / 28 mi to the south. A saltwater lagoon has formed between two spits of land that connect the island to the mainland. The **INSIDER TIP** sandy beach at the southern spit *Feniglia (www.tuttomaremma. com/riservadunafeniglia.htm,* bicycle hire on the guarded car parks) is protected by a wide stretch of pine trees which can only be reached on foot or by bike.

The old harbour village of *Orbetello* – on a headland, which juts from the mainland into the lagoon – is connected to the foothills by an artificial dam. It has a noteworthy cathedral and a rustic fish restaurant, *I Pescatori* (during summer open at lunch-

Wellness for free: A relaxing bath in the tufa pools near Saturnia

time, winter closed Mon–Thu | *Via Leopardi 9* | *tel. 05 64 86 06 11* | *Moderate*) run by local fishermen, where you can also buy the smoked fish eggs speciality INSIDER TIP *bottarga*.

In July and August, you can enjoy spectacular views of the coast completely free of charge in the INSIDER TIP beach shuttles *Navetta Spiagge:*, which tour the coast on several routes. Hop on in the harbour of *Porto Santo Stefano* at the start of the ❀ *Strada Panoramica*, lean back at the window and enjoy the view over the cliffs onto the turquoise sea. Hungry for more? Take another tour – it's

free! PDF with itinerary: *short.travel/tos5*. The family-friendly *Antica Fattoria La Parrina* (12 rooms, 4 apartments | district La Parrina | *tel. 05 64 86 26 36* | *www.parrina.it* | *Moderate–Expensive*) is a historic farm hotel near Albinia.

## PITIGLIANO ⭐
(159 F2) (*M17*)

When this village (pop. 4000) emerges suddenly (70 km / 43.5 mi to the south-east) it takes your breath away. It seems to grow right out the 300 m / 980 ft high tuff rock ridge that is stands on. Its 3500 year old history has been written by the Etruscans, the Romans and – during the Middle Ages – by the aristocratic Orsini family. The town centre, behind the massive aqueduct, is a labyrinth of alleys and stairs, where in the Middle Ages Spanish Jews found refuge. Reminders of this are INSIDER TIP the *cemetery*, a *synagogue* and a *museum* (April–Sept Sun–Fri 10am–1pm and 2.30pm–6pm, Oct–March 10am–noon and 3pm–5pm | *5 euros* | *Vicolo Marghera*) as well as a *pastry shop* (Via Zuccarelli 167) with kosher delicacies. The restaurant *Il Grillo* (Closed Tue | *Via Cavour 18* | *tel. 05 64 61 52 02* | *Budget–Moderate*) specialises in hearty traditional dishes.

## INSIDER TIP SATURNIA
(159 E2) (*L17*)

People come here for the hot sulphur springs that bubble out of the volcanic crater, 60 km / 37 mi east of Grosseto. The luxury hotel *Terme di Saturnia* built around the Roman spa (140 rooms | Follonata district | *tel. 05 64 60 01 11* | *www.termedisaturnia.it* | *Expensive*) also welcomes paying day visitors. The flowing water cascades into a ● waterfall, *Cascata del Mulino,* flowing in stages into a natural stone basin where you can enjoy its benefits free of charge.

### SORANO (159 F1–2) (*M16*)

Carved into rock this medieval village (pop. 3700) 80 km / 50 mi east of Grosseto is one of the most impressive that the south-east of Tuscany has to offer. It is terraced around a massive rock, and each of its narrow, winding streets, with residential towers and picturesque courtyards, is worth exploring. In the thick walls of the *castle* (built around 1550) that towers over the village, is the atmospheric *Hotel della Fortezza* (16 rooms | Piazza Cairoli 5 | tel. 05 64 63 35 49 | www.fortezzahotel.it | *Budget*). The rooms seem to be hovering on the brink of the abyss, but they are fit for a prince.

### SOVANA ★ (159 F2) (*M17*)

Wars and catastrophes left the village in a state of neglect, but the careful modernization and preservation of buildings have brought it back to life again. The small, classy hotel *Scilla* (15 rooms | Via Rodolfo Siviera 3 | tel. 05 64 61 41 13 | www.albergoscilla. com | *Budget*) on the cobbled village square is steeped in historic charm. In the 11th century the Aldobrandeschi family expanded the original Etruscan settlement into a gigantic fortress. Do not miss out on the village's Romanesque *cathedral* as well as the ● *Parco Archeologico Città del Tufo (March Sat / Sun 10am–5pm, April–Sept daily 10am–7pm, Oct daily 10am–6pm | 5 euros | www. leviecave.it)* on the SP 22 in the direction of San Martino. There you will find the 3rd century tomb *Tomba Ildebranda* with its columns and stairs hewn into the rock, as well as *Il Cavone*, a deep road carved into the soft tuff stone. Take home some Etruscan culture in the form of jewellery reproductions from *Arte Etrusca (Closed Wed | Via del Duomo 24)*.

# LIVORNO

(148 B3–4) (*D9*) **The people of Livorno are a merry folk; their local dialect has a distinctive twang, reminiscent of American English. It is the language of seafarers, the result of the meeting of many cultures and traditions. The Livornese sense of humour is legendary – many Italian comedians come here for inspiration. The citizen's sense of place is a charming paradox: For them, there is no city more beautiful than Livorno (pop. 157,000). But if you ask them why tourism is not more apparent here, they act surprised that you think that there should be.**

Livorno truly is a well-kept secret. The lively yet humble seaport does not boast the pomp of the renaissance nor will you find winding medieval alleyways here. Instead, the streets and piazzas are broad and sunlit. Livorno came into its own in the 16th century, when the powerful Medici clan needed access to the sea. And in order to attract wealthy Jewish merchants to the city, the freedom of speech and religion was established early on.

> **CITY** **WHERE TO START?**
> Start with a stroll along the seaside promenade **Viale Italia**. You can leave your vehicle at the parking area (with costs) on the Piazza Mazzini in front of the Nuova Darsena docks and take the bus no. 1 to the Mascagni observation platform and to the aquarium. In the opposite direction, bus line no. 1 goes to the central Piazza Grande, from where you can comfortably reach the Quartiere Venezia and the two Medici fortresses.

A channel connects the Old and New fortress of Livorno

## SIGHTSEEING

### FORTEZZA VECCHIA AND FORTEZZA NUOVA

Back in the 16th century, the two brick fortresses served as outposts to secure the seaport of the rich and powerful Medici clan. Nowadays, the *Fortezza Vecchia* is a busy event venue; there is something going on here almost every summer evening. Every year during the *Effetto Venezia (www.livornoeffettovenezia.it)*, a major music festival taking place in July, the entire city district of Venezia Nuova will he heaving with visitors from all over the globe listening to jazz, indie and rock music.

The *Fortezza Nuova* is now a major park where the locals come for their lunch break or take a leisurely evening stroll to enjoy the lovely view over the battlements. The park is also a favorite haunt of the poets, authors or artists of the region who ply their various trades for the enjoyment of locals and visitors alike.

### LUNGOMARE

As soon as the sun appears this 4 km / 2.5 mi long seaside promenade – between the bathing beach Scoglia della Regina and the circular pine grove Rotonda Ardenza – fills up with pedestrians, cyclists and joggers. Along the way are the ☆ *Mascagni panorama terrace,* art nouveau villas, bars and cafés. In the evening the promenade is full of people strolling leisurely along.

### INSIDER TIP ► MUSEO CIVICO GIOVANNI FATTORI

During the 19th century the local painter Giovanni Fattori was a leading member of the "Macchiaioli", a Tuscan group of artists that like the French Impressionists resisted the dominant academic style. Artworks by Fattori and other group member are on display in the art nouveau Villa Mimbelli. *Tue–Sun 10am–1pm and 4pm–7pm | 6 euros | Via San Jacopo in Acquaviva*

### QUARTIERE VENEZIA NUOVA

The old district of merchants and fishermen is the heart of the town. Here, the *gozzi*, the traditional rowing boats emerge from the network of ancient canals to commence their daily training in the harbour basin. From the harbour, another network of tunnels reaches the buildings' foundations. In the old days, the riches of the city were stored here but today, the tunnels are occupied by studios and bars, such as INSIDER TIP *La Bodeguita (Mon closed | Scali Finocchietti 28 | Tel. 34 66 10 08 32 | Budget.* During the day, you can sample the traditional local fare, and in the evenings, there is dance under the colonnades. You can explore the teeming life on top of Venezia Nuova's wooden foundations by boat: *Giro in Battello (10 euros | tickets in the Punto Informazioni | Via Pieroni 18 | www.livornoinbattello.info).*

## FOOD & DRINK

### ANTICA TORTERIA DA GAGARIN

For the best *cecina* – a delicious local pancake made from chickpea flour – in town. Try this snack bar behind the market hall. *Mon–Sat 8am–2pm and 4.30pm–8.30pm | Via Cardinale 24 | Budget*

### L'OSTRICAIO

Excellent seafood, a fantastic atmosphere and fair prices are a sure-fire guarantee that the small shack on the beach promenade is always full to the rafters. *Daily | Viale Italia 100 | Tel. 05 86 58 13 45 | Moderate*

## SHOPPING

### BOTTEGA CAMPAGNA AMICA ◎

A local cooperative specializing in the direct selling of regionally sourced food. *(Mon–Sat 9am–1pm and 5pm–8pm | Piazza dei Legnami 22)*

### MARKETS

Do try to prise your eyes away from the mouth-watering local delicacies of the 180-odd market stalls for long enough to admire the imposing art nouveau cast iron and stone construction of the ● *Mercato Centrale (Mon–Sat 7.30am–1.30pm | Via del Cardinale/Via Buontalenti).* Unlike the Central Market, INSIDER TIP *Mercatino Americano (Mon–Sat 10am–7pm | Via della Cinta Esterna/Piazzale del Portuale)* still feels like a temporary post-war structure. But the countless stalls of local handicraft and foreign imports are a veritable treasure trove for collectors and bargain hunters.

## SPORTS & ACTIVITIES

### CYCLING

Avoid the stress of traffic or public transport and hire a comfortable city bicycle and explore Livorno along its cycle paths and the miles and miles of seaside promenade. Download the *BicinCittà* app, and for 5 euros a day, the city is your oyster! You can find and abandon the bicycles at nine strategically positioned bicycle stations in town. *www.bicincitta.com*

## ENTERTAINMENT

### BAR CIVILI

Artists paid for their *ponce*, a local beverage made with coffee and rum, with paintings which now decorate the walls of the restaurant. *Closed Sun | Via della Vigna 55*

## WHERE TO STAY

### GRAND HOTEL PALAZZO

Here the glorious belle époque era continues in the 21st century but the comforts are all very modern. *123 rooms | Viale Italia 195 | tel. 05 86 26 08 36 | www.grandhotelpalazzo.it | Moderate–Expensive*

### HOTEL AL TEATRO

This mid range hotel impresses with its central location and beautiful courtyard where you can breakfast during summer. Garage parking possible. *8 rooms | Via Enrico Mayer 42 | tel. 05 86 89 87 05 | www.hotelalteatro.it | Moderate*

## INFORMATION

*Via Pieroni 18–20 | tel. 05 86 89 42 36 | www.costadeglietruschi.it*

## WHERE TO GO

### CASTIGLIONCELLO (148 B5) *(∅ D11)*

This village (pop. 3500), 27 km / 16 mi to the south was once a fashionable bathing resort during the 19th century, when Florentine nobles built their summer villas on the cliffs with private access to the bays. During the 1970s and 1980s it was the meeting place for Rome's jet-set crowd. Today the summer fun has been democratised, albeit with very high prices. There is a very beautiful ⚲ coastal promenade that goes to the neighbouring village Rosignano.

### MARINA DE CECINA, MARINA DI CASTAGNETO CARDUCCI AND BOLGHERI (148 C6, 154 A–B 1–2) *(∅ E–F 11–12)*

The seaside resorts along the *Costa degli Etruschi* are famously family-friendly. There is something her for everyone: The teenagers can go snorkelling along the rocky coast, mum can spend the entire day sunbathing on the sandy beaches while dad cycles along the long and sunny beach promenades while the grandparents watch the smaller members of the family having fun at the pony games for children.

If you crave more activity and a good glass of wine, you can help to harvest the grapes at one of the local vineyards. And in the evening, the whole family comes together on the sandy beach terrace of *La Tana del Pirata (May–Sept daily | Via Milano 17 | tel. 05 65 74 41 43 | www.latanadelpirata.com | Moderate–Expensive)* to enjoy the restaurant's delicious seafood under the starry sky.

And if you need a change from the beach, take a trip down the 5 km / 3 mi long cypress avenue leading up to the fortified wall of the medieval village of ★ *Bolgheri* huddled around the impressive castle of the Gherardesca: a symphony in green and, behind the archway, a crescendo and finale in red! The village may be a tiny bit touristy, but do try the *Taverna del Pittore (Closed Mon | Largo Nonna Lucia 4 |tel. 05 65 76 21 84 | Moderate–Expensive):* local cuisine, served on the terrace in the summer and in the winter, in a room with a cosy fireplace.

### MUSEO DELLA GEOTERMIA DI LARDERELLO (155 D1) *(∅ G12)*

Some 85 km / 50 mi south-east of Livorno is the world's oldest geothermal plant with a network of metal tubes where hot steam from the earth is converted into electricity. The plant's museum documents the history of this pioneering sustainable energy plant. *Mid-March–Oct daily 9.30am–6.30pm, Nov–mid-March Tue–Sun 10am–5pm | free admission | Piazza Leopolda | www.museivaldicecina.it*

### PARCO ARCHEOLOGICO DI BARATTI E POPULONIA ★ ● (154 A4) (𝄞 E14)

The medieval Populonia, 75 km / 46.5 mi to the south of Livorno, on a rocky ledge above the INSIDER TIP *Gulf of Baratti,* was an important Etruscan iron smelting centre. Their kilns were situated down on the coast. When researchers removed layers of slag during the 20th century, they found necropolises, tombs and workshops. Today the site is accessible as an *Archaeology Park (March–May and Oct Tue–Sun 10am–5pm, June and Sept 10am–7pm, July/Aug daily 9.30am–7.30pm Nov–Feb Sat/Sun 10am–5pm | 15 euros, Nov–Feb 9 euros | www.parchival dicornia.it).* The wide sweeping bay with fine white sand and crystal clear water is one of the most beautiful beaches in Tuscany. Large umbrella pines provide shade, fishing boats bob in the small harbour, and still you only have to pay for the parking, not to swim. Exquisite grilled fish dishes and tasty desserts are served at the summer restaurant *I Tretruschi (daily | tel. 0 56 52 93 80 | www.itretruschi. it | Moderate)* directly next to the excavation sites of Baratti.

### SAN VINCENZO (154 A3) (𝄞 E13)

The seaside resort (pop. 7000) bursts at its seams during summer. It has lovely sandy beaches, great holiday resorts, a yacht marina and a wide selection of leisure activities. A former school that has been converted into an elegant apartment hotel with swimming pool, *Residenza Santa Cecilia (15 apartments | Via dell'Asilo 2 | tel. 05 65 70 74 57 | www. santa-cecilia.it | Expensive)* is excellent value for money. *Il Cantuccio (Mon closed | Via Biserno 11 | tel. 05 65 70 20 20 | Moderate)* is a good address for the whole family offering pizza for the kids and tasty local food, including fish, for the adults at modest prices.

In the shade of the pine trees and crystal clear water: the park at Baratti and Populonia

# LUCCA, PISA & VERSILIA

Charming Lucca (with its lovely Garfagnana countryside), Massa Carrara (between the sea and the Apuan Alps) and Pisa (the former naval superpower on the alluvial plain of the Arno River mouth): The three provinces in the north-west have shaped the fate of the entire region. They owe their fortune to the trade along the medieval pilgrimage route, the Via Francigena, which connected Francia with Rome.

## LUCCA

(144 C5) *(∅ E7)* The 4 km/2.5 mi long and 12 m/40 ft high city wall of Lucca (pop. 87,000) encircles the city like "a sweet wrapper": Inside, it is filled to the brim with boutiques, hotels, trattorias,

**CITY** **WHERE TO START?**
Leave your car at the Carducci car park at the **Porta Sant'Anna**, and start with a stroll on top of the tree-lined city wall. Walking in a clockwise direction after 1 mile you will reach the Porto Santa Maria, where you can descend. Here you will find the tourism office and, a little further to the west, the San Frediano basilica. Take the Via Cavallerizza to the oval Piazza dell'Anfiteatro and a little further south to the watchtower, the Torre Guinigi, which is surrounded by holm oaks.

World famous images: the Leaning Tower of Pisa, Lucca's preserved city walls, marble quarries and the belle époque's bathing culture

**the city administration, the prison, red brick palazzi, apartment buildings, music schools, piazzas, museums, the University and umpteen churches.**

Lucca is a veritable labyrinth: you will find something new behind every corner - secret gardens, cosy restaurants, shops that sell local food or household goods, and of course lots and lots of chatting locals. It is a colourful melange of the middle ages and the renaissance with a bit of last century thrown in, and tourists from all over and locals going about their day.

Just forget the map and walk (or even better, cycle) where your whim takes you. Allow yourself to get lost because no matter where you go you will always end up at the city wall.

LE MURA

Between the walls, Lucca is buzzing with life: people, cyclists, athletes, gardens, children, play areas and in the summer, street art. Below all that, to the left of the

Porta San Pietro, there is the underworld of battlements, dark and shady arches fit for secret Casanovas and phantoms.

### MUSEO NAZIONALE PALAZZO MANSI

The autonomous city of Lucca became rich through the silk trade. The Palazzo of the Mansi family is a prime example for the over-the-top ostentatiousness so fashionable during the silk merchant's heyday in the Middle Ages. *Tue–Sat 8.30am–7.30pm | 4 euros | Via Galli Tassi 43*

that once stood on this spot. Then, busy merchants sold fish and produce under its arches and today, the city is still bubbling like fresh Lucchese fish soup in a merry hubbub of shopper and sightseers among cafes and restaurants. Nowadays, the market stalls fetch premium rents.

### SAN FREDIANO

The church next to the city wall was consecrated in 1147; it has a charming interior with a marble altar (1422) by Jacopo della

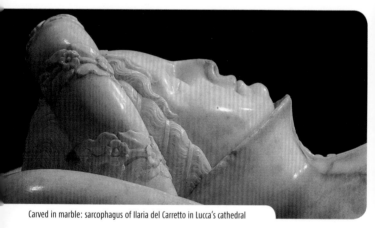

Carved in marble: sarcophagus of Ilaria del Carretto in Lucca's cathedral

### INSIDER TIP ▶ PALAZZO PFANNER

Instead of nectar, the fountains should have been flowing with beer – for in the 19th century, this was the property of the Pfanners, a family of brewers who built this paradise of citrus trees, colourful flowers, bubbling fountains and ornamental parts for their private enjoyment. You can stay in the sumptuous mansion from €100 per night. *April–Oct daily 10am–6pm | Nov 11am–4pm | 6 euros | Via degli Asili 33 | www.palazzopfanner.it*

### PIAZZA DELL'ANFITEATRO ★

Every Labyrinth has a centre - in this case, it is the oval of a Roman amphitheatre

Quercia and a decorated Romanesque baptismal font. The mosaic on the façade depicts Christ's ascension. *Daily 9am–noon and 3pm–5pm, in the summer until 6pm | Piazza San Frediano*

### SAN MARTINO

Ilaria del Carretto must have been beloved by all, judging from her marble sarcophagus so lovingly created by Jacopo della Quercia in 1408. The Princess was the perfect wife – stately, beautiful and kind, peacefully awaiting resurrection atop her grave in marble effigy. She had died giving birth after having dutifully given her lord a son. Another notable site in the Romanesque Cathedral is the *Volto Santo*, the so-called "Face of Jesus". In the 12th century, thousands of pilgrims used to come to Lucca to see the wooden relic, which is still carried around the city in a solemn procession each September. *Summer Mon–Fri 9.30am–6pm, Sat 9.30am–6.45pm, Sun 9–10am and 11.45am–6.45pm, winter Mon–Fri 9.30am–5pm, Sat 9.30am–6pm, Sun 11.30–5pm | Piazza San Martino*

### SAN MICHELE IN FORO

This church at the former Roman forum was built during the 12th century. It has a remarkable five-storey marble façade of blind arches with a statue of St Michael on top. The building is considered one of the most beautiful Romanesque buildings in Tuscany and also has a rich interior by the likes of Andrea della Robbia and Filippino Lippi. *Daily 8am–noon and 3pm–6pm | Piazza San Michele*

### TORRE GUINIGI

The palazzo of the Luccanese merchant clan Guinigi is the only one which still boasts a tower – and there are trees growing on it! According to old records, holm oaks have been growing on the tower since the 15th century. *Daily 9.30am–4.30pm, March and Oct until 5.30pm, Apr/May until 6.30pm, Jun–Sept until 7.30pm | 4 euros | Via Sant'Andrea 45*

## FOOD & DRINK

### INSIDER TIP ▶ OSTERIA DA GIOMO ⋇

The food makes you enjoy the view even more. Once you have entered this restaurant in Valgiono, you will never want to leave! Thursday is fish day. You can get there by car (12 km/7.5 mi to the northeast), the Vaibus from Piazzale Verde or by taxi. Booking recommended. *Closed for lunchtime and Mon, winter also closed Tue | Via di Mezzo 3 | Valgiano | tel. 34 08 56 26 75 | Budget–Moderate*

### TRATTORIA DA LEO

Popular lunch restaurant serving good, reasonably priced home-style cooking. *Daily | Via Tegrimi 1 | tel. 05 83 49 22 36 | Budget–Moderate*

### LA TANA DEL BOIA

Nice atmosphere, tasty *panini* and excellent microbrewery beer – this snack bar offers everything rolled into one. *Closed Mon | Piazza San Michele 37*

## SHOPPING

### INSIDER TIP ▶ ANTICHE TESSITURE LUCCHESI

Get your fancy (silken) threads – or learn how to make them yourself - in Palazzo

---

### MARCO POLO HIGHLIGHTS

★ **Campo dei Miracoli in Pisa**
The "field of miracles" around the Leaning Tower → p. 96

★ **Piazza dell'Anfiteatro in Lucca**
So often seen in photographs – the famous oval piazza is unmistakable → p. 86

★ **Pietrasanta**
A Mecca for sculptors throughout the ages → p. 94

★ **Pontremoli**
Elegant town on the green slopes of the Apennines → p. 95

★ **Passeggiata in Viareggio**
An art déco town from the early days of the bathing culture → p. 96

Mansi! The atelier of Genni Tommasi and her crew of co-workers in the medieval rooms is a treasure trove of delicate scarves, shawls and dresses, all hand-made and designed according to the old tradition of silk and brocade weaving.

### ANTICA BOTTEGA DI PROSPERO

Straight out of a bedtime story: a shop full of shining cellophane packets, bulging sacks and bulbous ceramic vats, the aroma of all olive oil chestnut flour and the succulent Bazzone ham from the Garfangnana – presided over by the avuncular shopkeeper with shining steel framed spectacles. *Via Santa Lucia 13*

### MERCATO DELL'ANTIQUARIATO

The antiques market that takes place around the cathedral square every third weekend of the month has been running for almost 50 years.

## SPORTS & ACTIVITIES

The steep slopes of Lucca's environs are a favourite training area for professional cyclists. The *Biogiro (www.biogirogesam. it)* has a few challenging slopes as well but wends its hilly way past osterias and stately mansions. If you want company, you can book a hiking or cycling tour with nature guide Serena Scalici at *www.eco-guide.it.* You can also book different types of bicycles as well as electric bicycles for 3 euros an hour or 15 euros a day at *Cicli Bizzarri (Piazza Santa Maria 32 | tel. 05 83 49 66 82 | www.ciclibizzarri.net)*

## ENTERTAINMENT

Just follow the crowd! A typical evening starts at the Porta dei Borghi between Via Fillungo and Via Michele Rosi with a craft beer, a glass of wine or a cocktail. Then you have three choices: stay here, move on to the *Caffè del Mercato (Closed Sun | Piazza San Michele 17 | live music and shows in the summer)* for a INSIDER TIP *pechino,* a mysterious cocktail of 10 different liqueurs created by bartender Andrea every week), or in the summer to a beach bar, for example on the Lido di Camaiore or Viareggio.

## WHERE TO STAY

### ANFITEATRO B & B

The best setting, cosy atmosphere and great value for money make this B & B a hidden gem. *5 rooms, 5 suites, 4 apartments | Via Anfiteatro 25 | tel. 33 83 70 74 83 | www.anfiteatrolucca.it | Moderate*

### ALBERGO CELIDE

Friendly hotel right next to the city wall with individually decorated rooms, its own seafood restaurant and large outdoor terrace. Bicycles available to hotel guests at no charge. *48 rooms | Viale Giuseppe Giusti 25 | tel. 05 83 95 41 06 | www.albergocelide.it | Moderate*

## INFORMATION

*Vecchia Porta San Donato* and *Piazzale Verdi | tel. 05 83 58 31 50 | www.luccaitinera.it*

## WHERE TO GO

### BAGNI DI LUCCA (145 D3) (*∅ F6*)

Start the day with a bath in the hot thermal springs followed by a shower in the grotto, then on into the steam room, punctuated by frequent drinking breaks, with pure spring water naturally. Back in the day, the wealthy patrons frequenting the thermal baths would spend their evenings in Europe's first gambling casino. Today, the erstwhile splendour has faded, and the building is now home to the tourist information: *Via Umberto 103 | tel. 0583 80 57 45 | www.prolocobagnidilucca.it*. On the other hand, using the thermal baths has become very affordable and the view of the valley with its little rivers, sources and lakes is a wellness break for the eyes. Enjoy a sumptuousmeal at a reasonable prices in the INSIDER TIP *Circolo dei Forestieri (Closed Tue | Piazza Jean Varraud 10 | tel. 0583 86 0 38 | Moderate)*.

### BARGA (144 C2) (*E5*)

The breathtaking views of the Apuan Alps from the *Piazzale Arringo* and the 12th century *San Cristofano Cathedral* – with the light filtering through the alabaster framed windows onto a 1000 year old figure of Christopher and a marble pulpit supported by lions – make the 35 km / 21.5 mi trip north to the mountain town (pop. 10,000) worthwhile. When strolling through the streets you will be surprised by the beautiful Renaissance buildings which date back to a time when silk production was the centre of the town's existence.

### GARFAGNANA (144 B–C 1–2) (*D–E 4–5*)

The soft rolling hills of the Apennines in the east, the craggy mountains of the Apuan Alps in the west and in between pristine valleys, chestnut forests, and picturesque villages: this is the exceptionally beautiful Serchio River valley north of Lucca. The best way to explore it is the gentle way: a hike on the 110 km / 68 mi long loop trail or a walk on a bridle path – signposted *ippovie*.

If this is all too idyllic for you: In the *Vagli Park (daily 9am–6pm | single jump 49 euros/pers., double jump 40 euros/pers., booking through the website only | wwwvaglipark.it)* near Vagli Sotto, you can board one of the few INSIDER TIP Megaziplines in Europe, aptly named Volo degli Angeli, "flight of the angels". But these angels fly devilishly fast: alone or in pairs, holding hands or clutching each other (and with or without plastic wings) you zip down a 2 km / 1.2 mi long steel cable at 150 km/h (93 mi/h) as the wind whips back your hair and the moun-

The picturesque village of Barga before the backdrop of the Alpi Apuane

tains zip by below you. Goodbye mountaineering, hello ziplining!

Below the mountain, take a walk among the sparkling stalactites and stalagmites and subterranean lakes of the *Grotta del Vento (April–Nov daily, Dec–March Mon–* produce and gossip. On the way back to Lucca, do stop to look at the weirdly shaped "devil's bridge", the *Ponte del Diavolo in Borgo a Mozzano*, a favourite hangout for ghosts and monsters each November at Halloween.

A twitcher's catwalk: A walkway through the reeds of Lago di Massaciuccoli

*Sat 10am–4pm, admission on the hour | 9/14/20 euros depending on the tour | www.grottadelvento.com)* The grotto's entrance area is a fairyland in its own right, for the wind has formed the rugged, karstic rocks into shapes resembling gnomes and enchanted creatures. On the way to the grotto, trattorias and market stalls offer regional specialties, for instance products made from INSIDER**TIP** products from chestnut flour. Before you enter the winding access road to the grotto near Gallicano, take a short detour to the INSIDER**TIP** *Calomini hermitage (www.eremocalomini.com)*, which hangs like a balcony from the steep cliff wall. The Thursday *market* in the old town of the main village of *Castelnuovo di Garfagnana* is the place to go for local

Information: *Piazza delle Erbe 1 | Castelnuovo di Garfagnana | tel. 0 58 36 51 69 | www.turismo.garfagnana.eu*

### LAGO DI MASSACIUCCOLI
(144 B5) *(Ø D7)*

The shallow lake with its broad band of reeds is a residue of the delta lagoon that was here a century ago. The wetlands are breeding grounds for migratory birds, and form part of the *Parco Regionale di Migliario, San Rossore, Massaciuccoli* reserve and can be explored via footpaths and walkways on stilts. On the banks is *Torre del Lago* (pop. 11,000) where the composer Giacomo Puccini once lived. Today his home is a *museum (Tue–Sun 10am–12.40pm and 3–5.20pm, Mon 3–5.20pm | Apr–Nov until 6.20pm |*

*7 euros | Belvedere Puccini | www.giaco mopuccini.it).* His works are performed annually from mid-July until late August during the *Puccini Festival (www.puccini festival.it)* on an impressive floating stage. During the summer the town is a popular gay meeting spot *(www.friendlyversilia. it).*

### VILLE LUCCHESI (144 C4–5) *(Ø E–F7)*

The splendid country mansions of the patrician families dot the surrounding hills. Two of many examples: the *Villa Torrigiani (March–Oct daily 10am–1pm and 3–5pm, June–Sept until 6.30pm | 12 euros | Via del Gomberaio 3 | www.villeepalazzilucchesi. net)* in *Camigliano* 10 km / 6 mi east which enchants with its landscaped garden full of grottos, fountains and statues, and the *Villa Reale (March–Nov daily 10am–6pm | 9 euros | Viale Europa | www.parcovilla reale.it)* in *Marlia* 10 km / 6 mi northeast with its open air boxwood theatre set in a baroque garden.

# MASSA

*(143 D5) (Ø C5–6)* **After a pleasant morning climbing around in the marble quarry, there is nothing better than feeling the hot sand between your toes and enjoying the view of the marble face shining brightly from between the rugged cliffs above. In the evening, watching the sun go down from Castello Malaspina in the old town is a must.**

M stands for Massa, for marble – this is the world's largest extraction site, having supplied artists and artisans with first-rate material for centuries, for Marina di Massa, which boasts one of the longest sand beaches of the region – and for Malaspina, the noble family that shaped the appearance of the town (pop 70,000) for more than 300 years.

### CASTELLO MALASPINA ⋰⋱

In 800 the castle was used as a impenetrable retreat for the city rulers, at its high point it is only accessible via a narrow staircase lane. The view of the city, coast and mountains will take your breath away. The Malaspina family, who lived here since 1442 used the Renaissance castle (15th century) as their stately seat (today it is a museum). *June–Sept Tue–Sun 10.30am–1pm and 5.30–11pm, Oct–May Sun 2.30–6.30pm | 5.50 euros | Via del Forte 15 | www. comune.massa.ms.it*

### SANTI PIETRO E FRANCESCO

The cathedral has a beautiful marble façade and double loggias, one on top of each other and its splendid baroque interior houses the Malaspina family tombs. *Daily 9am–7pm | Via Dante*

### IL FORNARETTO

Nobody will go hungry hungry with Umberto's INSIDER TIP ▶ *pizza lunga.* The largest one, which is 2,20 m / 7.2 ft long, can feed the entire clan. And Mamma Anna is cooking up a storm. *Closed Mon and lunchtime | Via Castagnara 187 | tel. 05 85 83 15 36 | www.pizzeriailfornaretto. it | Moderate*

### LA PÉNICHE

Cormorants are looking on in disbelief as you are dining on their dinner, floating on a pontoon in Massa di Marina. Besides local fish, La Péniche specialises in all the good things the region has to offer: Colonnata bacon, saffron courgettes and truffle ravioli. *Daily | Via Lungo Brugiano 3 | tel. 05 85 24 01 17 | www. lapeniche.com | Moderate*

## SHOPPING

**CASA DEL VIMINE DAL 1963**

There is hardly more than a handful of basket weavers left in Europe. But one Massa family is still plying the ancient trade and you can also take courses with them. You may wish you had a larger car when you visit their workshop. *Mon/Wed/Fri 9am–4.30pm | Via Beatrice 2/Via Alberica 35*

## ENTERTAINMENT

**BEACH CLUB VERSILIA**

Ranked for years as Versilia's best nightlife spot in summer where you can dine and then dance off the calories. *Summer daily, otherwise Fri–Sun | Viale IV Novembre 18 | Cinquale district | www.beachclub versilia.it*

## WHERE TO STAY

**HOTEL GABRINI**

Family run three star hotel on the coast in Marina di Massa. Large garden, 45 comfortable rooms, garage. *Via Luigi Sturzo 19 | tel. 05 85 24 05 05 | www.hotelgabrini.it | Moderate*

## INFORMATION

*Lungomare Vespucci 24 | Marina di Massa | tel. 05 85 24 00 63 | www.turismomas sacarrara.it*

## WHERE TO GO

**APUAN ALPS**

(143 D–F 4–6) (ØØ C–D 5—6)

The mountain range rises up to 2000 m / 656 ft from the Tyrrhenian Sea. On the coastal side lemon trees bloom during winter, while in the interior snow lingers in the valleys until May. As compensation, rare wild mouflon sheep cavort in the woods and golden eagles nest in the cliffs. The INSIDER TIP *Orto Botanico Pietro Pellegrini (June–beginning of Sept daily 9am–1pm and 3–7pm | 3 euros | booking: tel. 05 85 49 03 49 | aquilegia17@gmail. com | www. parcapuane.it/ob)* near *Pian della Fioba* is an excellent introduction to the region. The winding path climbs through lemon trees up through several zones of vegetation; rare, colourful orchids on the left and the steep precipice on the right. This is why during the one-hour tour, you will always be in the company of an experienced guide. If you book soon enough, you may even catch an English-speaking guide. More ambitious hikers will enjoy the nature reserve *Parco Regionale delle Alpi Apuane (www.parca puane.it).* More information in the visitor's centre, *Centro Visite (Via Corrado del Greco 11 | tel. 0 58 47 58 21)* in Seravezza and in Castelnuovo di Garfagnana *(Fortezza di Mont'Alfonso | tel. 05 83 64 44 78).*

On the way up into the mountains, be sure to visit the remote hamlet of

## LOW BUDGET

*Incaba (Tue–Sat 9.30am–12.30pm and 3.30–8pm, Sun 4–8pm | Via Provinciale 241)* is a wholesale market on the outskirts of Camaiore that sells children's products. Prices are 20 to 40 per cent less than elsewhere in Europe.

The *Outlet Atelier D'Avenza (Mon/Tue/Thu/Fri 9am–1pm and 3–6pm, Wed/Sat 9am–1pm | Via Aurelia 22)* at the Carrara motorway exit in Avenza sells *alta moda* for men at almost half the price you would pay in the shops.

You've got to take the heat: working in the marble quarries of Carrara

INSIDER TIP *Peralta (4 rooms, 7 apartments | Via Pieve 321 | tel. 39 31 71 72 46 | www.peraltatuscany.com | Moderate).* where a Mexican artist has given the holiday cottage nestled between old walls, orchards and gazebos a true Latin American makeover, vibrant, joyful and relaxing at the same time!

## CARRARA (143 D5) *(ℳ C5)*

This city (pop. 64,000) is synonymous with snow white marble that is carved in workshops into art or souvenirs. The charming pedestrian area in the old town is relatively unknown, but there is a lot to discover: the Romanesque *cathedral* with its marble bell tower, the *fountain of Neptune* by Baccio Bandinelli next to it and of course the *marble museum Museo Civico del Marmo (Tue–Sun 10.30am–1.30pm and 4–7pm | 5 euros | Viale XX Settembre 85 | Stadio district).*

Enjoy coffee and cake in the *Drogheria Pasticceria Caflisch (Via Roma 2),* excellent fish dishes in the *Tavernetta da Franco* *(Closed Mon | Piazza Alberica 10 | tel. 05 85 77 77 82 | www.ristorantelatavernetta. it | Moderate).* For a pleasant, simple place to stay in the old town, try the B&B *Antica Carrara (5 rooms | Via dell'Arancio 17 | tel. 0 58 57 42 75 | Budget).*

## INSIDER TIP GROTTA ANTRO DEL CORCHIA ● (143 E5) *(ℳ D6)*

With 1500 grottos, caves and shafts, the Apuan Alps have more holes than Swiss cheese. Three of the caves are open to tourists, including this one in Levigliani di Stazzema, a giant cave with a labyrinth of tunnels. Two hour guided trips are available (departing in the village). *Variable opening times | 13 euros | Via IV Novembre 70 | www.antrocorchia.it*

## INSIDER TIP LUNIGIANA
(142 B–C 2–4) *(ℳ A–B 3–5)*

The Magra Valley in the extreme northwest of Tuscany is a quiet, remote area. In ancient times, pilgrims, merchants and soldiers carefully made their way through the dense woodlands, eyed with suspicion from the more than 100 castles of the region. Only very few of them are left today. In the castle of the *Malaspina in Fosdinovo (guided tours: summer Wed–Mon 11am, noon, 4pm, 5pm, 6pm, winter Sat/Sun 3pm, 4pm, 5pm, Sun also 11am,*

Stone Age Art: The famous statues of Lunigiana in Museum of Pontremoli

*noon | 6 euros | Via Papiriana 2 | www. castellodifosdinovo.it)* you can access your inner prince or poet: in the sumptuous four poster beds of the seven lordly guest rooms (*Moderate*), in the renaissance salon and on the sun terrace on top of the viewing tower. Meanwhile, the common people can take a tour of the dungeons, the torture chamber, the haunted room and the ☙ tower. Worth a detour (from Aulla via the SS 63) is the village of *Equi Terme* with its splendid dripstone cave, the *Grotte di Equi (changing opening*

*times | 8.50 euros | grottediequi.it).* Each Christmas, the grotto is turned into a live nativity scene. More information at *www. terredilfnigiana.com.*

## MARBLE QUARRIES IN COLONNATA AND FANTISCRITTI (143 D5) (*ill C5*)

For centuries people have been mining the white "stone of light" from the mountains above Carrara. An environmental disaster and yet the fascination with the quarry, the *cave,* continues. In Fantiscritti at Miseglia above Carrara *Marmotour (Mon–Fri 11am–5pm, May–Aug until 6.30pm, Sat / Sun 11am–6.30pm | 10 euros | Piazzale Fantiscritti 84 | www.mar motour.com)* organises tours into the impressive underworld. Do not forget your jacket! There is an *open air museum (April–Oct daily 9am–6pm | donations welcome | www.cavamuseo.com),* where displays of the different marble types and mining and transport methods are exhibited.

A few miles further in *Colonnata* you can find the much vaunted, delicate bacon *lardo di Colonnata,* at shops like *Marino Giannarelli (Via Comunale di Colonnata 2).* The pork back fat is seasoned and cured in marble vats for months. The best restaurant in the region is the *Locandapuana (Closed Sun evening and Mon | Via Comunale 1 | tel. 05 85 76 80 17 | www. locandaapuana.com | Moderate).*

## PIETRASANTA ★
(143 E6) (*ill C6*)

The charming fortified town (pop. 24,000), 12 km / 7.4 mi to the southeast, is a Mecca for sculptors and stonemasons. There is one marble workshop after another and you may browse – but only by appointment.One such place is the *Studio Pescarella (tel. 05 84 75 63 47 | www.studiopescarella.com).* Much of the old town is made from marble: its curbstones, benches and the *San Martino Cathedral*. Its brick bell tower is a lovely contrast. It is reached via the Via Garibaldi, past the hotel *Albergo Pietrasanta (20 rooms | Via Garibaldi 35 | tel. 05 84 79 37 26 | www.albergopietra santa.com | Expensive)*, the delicatessen shop *Antichi Sapori (Via Garibaldi 62)* and the *Pizzeria La Corte (Closed Mon | Via Giuseppe Garibaldi 55 | tel. 05 84 79 08 30 | Budget–Moderate)* which is praised for its wholemeal focaccia.

The seaside resort *Marina di Pietrasanta* offers a wide, sandy beach and an intense nightlife. Trendy meeting spots are the jetty at sundown or the bar of the Bagno Comunale *(Viale Roma 3)* on the northern edge of the town. The summer festival *La Versiliana (www.laversilianafestival.it)* adds a necessary dose of culture.

In the hinterland, the village of *Sant'Anna di Stazzema* gained notoriety in 1944 when SS henchmen massacred 540 civilians. The INSIDER TIP *Museo Storico della Resistenza (April–Sept Tue/Wed 9am–2pm, Thu–Sat 9am–6pm, Sun 10.30am–6.30pm | Oct–March Tue–Thu 9am–2pm, Fri/Sat 9am–5pm, Sun 2–6pm | free admission | www.santannadistazzema.org)* commemorates the event.

## PONTREMOLI ★ (142 B2) (*∅ A3*)

Beetle-shaped menhirs...? Knee-high, waist-high, shoulder-high, the standing stones are lined up in a row, weather-beaten images of human figures with tiny arms and legs that seem to have sprung from uneasy dreams. Enjoy this curious collection of ancient stelae in the *Museo delle Statue Stele Lunigianesi (June–Sept daily 10am–6.30pm, Aug until 7.30pm, Oct–May Tue–Sun 9.30am–5.30pm | 5 euros | www.statuestele.org)*. The elegant small town Pontremoli (pop. 7500) 60 km / 37 mi north of Massa seems far

removed from the hustle and bustle of the big cities; blissfully unknown to the wider world, life is going on here much as it always did among the arched colonnade and the old trattorias and cafes – try the *Caffè degli Svizzeri (Closed Mon | Piazza della Repubblica 21)*.

The town had its heyday as a waypoint along the Via Francigena. Today its wealth lies in the unspoilt nature that surrounds it, medicinal herbs, mushrooms, honey and cheese. In the *Osteria della Bietola (Closed Thu | Via Bietola 4 | tel. 01 87 83 19 49 | Budget–Moderate)* they know how to prepare all these treasures. Perfect relaxation in complete seclusion is guaranteed at the *Agriturismo Country-Hotel Costa d'Orsola (14 rooms | Orsola district | tel. 01 87 83 33 32 | www. costadorsola.it | Moderate)*.

## VERSILIA
### (143 D6, 144 A4–5) (*∅ C6–7*)

From May onwards, the entire Versilia coast becomes a holiday and party venue. During the day, you can live it up in one of the many beach bars along the coast where sun stretchers and umbrellas cover every square inch of the sand. In the evening, make the round of the beach clubs and the nightclubs in the towns *(disco techeinversilia.it)*. The INSIDER TIP *Vaibus (3.50 euros)* runs all night along the beach promenade, allowing easy access to open-air theatres, pubs and night clubs, for example the *Maki Maki* in Viareggio, the *Bussola Club* in Marina di Pietrasanta, the beach bars on the Lido di Camaiore and to the more discrete and sophisticated *Forte dei Marmi* in the North, the hangout of a more well-heeled clientele. They would also frequent the exquisitely refurbished art nouveau *Hotel Byron (29 rooms | Viale Ammiraglio Morin 46 | tel. 05 84 78 70 52 | www.hotelbyron.net | Expensive)*. But there is plenty of choice for all budgets. Get a good impression of Viareggio's erstwhile splendour while talking a walk south along the coast, which is still much as it always was.

### VIAREGGIO (144 A5) (*ⓜ C–D7*)

The oldest seaside resort in Italy (pop. 64,000), 25 km / 15.5 mi to the south-east), boasts a 3 km / 1.8 mile long ★ *Passeggiata* that runs straight between the pier in the south and the historic hotel Principe di Piemonte. It is crammed with bathing huts, hotels and splendid art nouveau villas with cafes, restaurants and boutiques. 200 years ago, Europe's high society brought the high life to this coast, filling the ancient seaport of Lucca with ornate palazzi, villas straight out of Arabian Nights and oriental pagodas. The circumstance may have vanished, but the pomp has not, and neither has the partying spirit. In February, everyone dons fanciful masks and costumes for Carnival. The ● *Museo del Carnevale (mid-June–mid-Sept Fri–Sun 9–11pm, Sat also 10am–noon, mid-Sept–mid-June Sat/Sun 4–7pm | 3 euros | Via Santa Maria Goretti | viareggio.ilcarnevale. com)* in the Cittadella del Carnevale is a phantasmagoria of mythical and fabulous creatures.

The INSIDER**TIP** *Villa Tina Hotel (14 rooms | Via Aurelio Saffi 2 | tel. 0 58 44 44 50 | www.villatinahotel.it | Moderate)* is a Belle Époque treasure with flowery stained-glass windows and gold friezes in the dining room. Don't miss the hall of mirrors in the Villa Argentina *(Tue–Sun 10am–1pm and 3–6.30pm | free admission | Via Amerigo Vespucci 44)*, which is now a cultural centre.

Fishermen also invite paying guests to sail out on their boats to catch local types of fish, the ● INSIDER**TIP** *pesce dimenticato*, or "forgotten fish", which are then prepared on board *(www.ittiturismo.it)*.

**WHERE TO START?**
At the **Campo dei Miracoli** (field of wonders) of course! You will need to leave your car outside of the city gates, for example in the car park next door in the *Via Cammeo C. Salomone 51*. If you'd prefer to travel by train, the best place to get off is at the Pisa San Rossore station. From the station it's just 500m/546 yards to the Campo dei Miracoli along the Via Bonanno Pisano.

# PISA

**MAP ON PAGE 98**
**(148 B2) (*ⓜ D8*) How the tables have turned: In the Middle ages, Pisa's fleet was notorious throughout the Mediterranean. Nowadays, the city (pop. 89,000) is being overrun by millions of tourists each year.**

Today, the object is not so much the city's riches, but rather something that went wrong with its architecture. Well, practically everyone is familiar with the image of the leaning tower of Pisa – is it really worth coming to have a look in person? Actually, yes! The university city at the River Arno with its pleasant gardens, impressive monuments and inviting piazzas has a pleasantly "studenty" atmosphere, yet few of the millions of visitors ever make it past the city's landmark...

## SIGHTSEEING

### CAMPO DEI MIRACOLI ★

It was intended to be an impressive demonstration of power, a "field of wonders": A cathedral, baptistery, bell tower and graveyard in gleaming white Carrara marble. Unfortunately, the alluvial soil

World famous by accident: the Duomo and the Leaning Tower of Pisa

at the city's west gate could not support the weight of the bell tower: It started to subside soon after construction started in 1173. In vain, the architects tried to compensate for the tower's tendency to lean. Luckily, the *torre pendente (18 euros, due to the limited number of visitors, advance booking recommended at www. opapisa.it, no children under 8 years)* is in no danger sinking further. It is worth coming to Pisa just to see the antics of the millions of tourists visiting the landmark: Hardly anyone can resist the temptation to have their picture taken while trying to prevent the tower from falling over. Don't let it bother you, try to get with the spirit – and do take the time to have a look around the other monuments, for they are really worth it. Apart from choosing the wrong subsoil to build on, the architects have done everything right. The tower, 100 Pisan cubits high (56 m/183 ft), with its narrow columns and delicate decorations, is a masterpiece of marble filigree.

In the *Duomo (free admission),* you can admire the best of many epochs and cultures: Byzantine mosaics under Romanesque arches (the cathedral was consecrated in 1118), a Gothic pulpit by Giovanni Pisano, which seems to be made up of writhing bodies; the massive, austere sepulchre of emperor Henry VII and the bronze candelabra which is said to have helped Galileo Galilei solve the mystery of the pendulum in the 16th century. Altar, baptismal font and surrounding walls of the Gothic baptistery opposite *(5 euros)* are covered in symmetrical lines and shapes that play havoc with the senses. In the graveyard, the *Camposanto (5 euros),* late antiquity reigns supreme. Originally, the sarcophagi had been positioned around the cathedral, where their frescoes sustained some damage during WW2. Opening times for all four monuments:

*March–Oct daily 10am–7pm, tower 9am–7pm, Nov–Feb 10am–5pm (cathedral 10am–1pm and 2–5pm).* If you prefer to visit more than one monument, opt for the cheaper multi-ticket *(www.opapisa.it).*

### MURALE DI PISA

Here the city shows that it is not stuck in history: in 1989 Keith Haring was commissioned to paint the wall of the Convento Sant'Antonio at the train station. The resulting mural is typical of his unique line drawings. *Via Riccardo Zandonai*

### ORTO BOTANICO

The botanical garden, one of the oldest in the world, was established in 1543 in order for the medical faculty to have medicinal plants for educational purposes. *April–Sept daily 8.30am–8pm, Oct–*

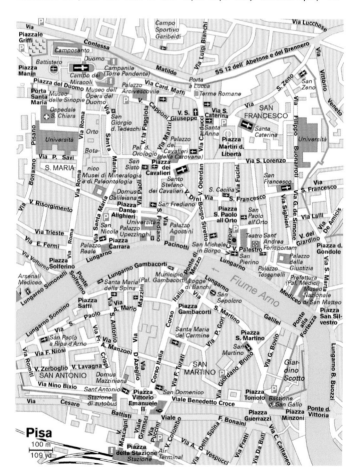

*March Mon–Sat 9am–5pm, Sun 9am–1pm | 4 euros | Via Luca Ghini 5*

### PIAZZA DEI CAVALIERI

Seven streets lead into this stately square, which was the centre of secular power during the Middle Ages. The *Palazzo dei Cavalieri* – which is decorated with sgraffito paintings and is very impressive – was radically redesigned in 1562 by Giorgio Vasari and today is the seat of the *Scuolo Normale Superiore* elite university.

### SANTA MARIA DELLA SPINA

This small stone church was built in 1230 on the edge of the Arno as a shrine for a thorn *(spina)* from Christ's crown. In 1871, when it was threatened by the rising Arno, it was dismantled and moved to higher ground. The building is a superb example of Gothic architecture. *March–Oct Tue–Sun 10am–2pm, April–Sept Tue–Fri also 3–6pm, Sat/Sun also 3–7pm | 2 euros | Lungarno Gambacorti*

What's the scoop? Gelato!

## FOOD & DRINK

### ANTICA TRATTORIA IL CAMPANO

Popular meeting spot for the locals, in the maze of the old town, that serves Tuscan dishes. *Closed Tue lunchtime, Thu lunchtime and Wed | Via Domenico Cavalca 19 | tel. 0 50 58 05 85 | www.ilcampano.com | Moderate*

### INSIDER TIP ► GELATERIA TUFFO 13 ⊘

This is the place for gelato aficionados: Hermetically closed iceboxes ensure that no preservatives are necessary. All ingredients are organic and there are interesting flavours: Try the beer ice cream! *Daily | Lungarno Gambacorti 13*

### LA SCALETTA

This traditional restaurant (founded in 1881!) is a must for gourmets. The presentation of each fish and seafood dish is a work of art in its own right. *Closed Sat lunchtime and Tue | Via Pietrasantina 107 | tel. 05 06 20 20 50 | www.ristorantelascalettapisa.com | Expensive*

## SHOPPING

### MERCATO DELLE VETTOVAGLIE

The food market, on the Piazza delle Vettovaglie with its ochre yellow houses, is an institution. *Mon–Sat mornings | Piazza delle Vettovaglie*

### PASTICCERIA SALZA

There are lots of elegant speciality shops on the Borgo Stretto and the sweet temptations in the traditional bakery at no. 46 are a must. *Closed Mon.*

## SPORTS & ACTIVITIES

### PISA WALKING TOURS

The two-hour long (English) guided tour takes you to the most remote corners of

Pisa. *16 euros | March–Oct daily on request 9.45am | The tour starts at the fountain in front of Pisa Centrale railway station | www.pisaexplorer.com*

### CYCLING
On a tandem or in a rickshaw, you will not lose sight of each other in all the hubbub. The brave ones can also rent single bicycles at *Toscana in Tour | from 14 euros/day | Via Uguccione della Faggiola 41 | tel. 33 32 60 21 52 | www.toscanaintour.it*

**INSIDER TIP** SUNSET CAFÉ
Beach bar in *Marina di Pisa* (15 km / 9 mi). Drinks and snacks are served on the beach and on weekends jazz or DJ music. *Summer daily 7pm–2am, Fri/Sat until 3am | Via Litoranea 40a | www.sunset-cafe.it*

### ENOTECA VICOLO DIVINO
Sommelière Martina specializes in smaller wineries. The wine is served along with *panini,* cheese and meat boards. *Closed Sun | Via Filippo Serafini 10 | www.vicolodivino.it*

**BED & BREAKFAST SAN MICHELE**
Fabrizio and Lucia make you feel at home in their no-frills B & B with garden located at the heart of the old town. *3 rooms | Via Cosimo Ridolfi 24 | tel. 0 50 57 02 67 | www.bedandbreakfast sanmichele.com | Budget*

### VILLA DI CORLIANO
Although the eleven rooms in this somewhat run-down baroque villa (11 km / 7 mi north in Rigoli) are simply furnished, that is offset by the fresco painted common room. *Strada Statale Abetone 50 | tel. 34 79 06 72 86 | www.villacorliano.it | Budget*

*Piazza Vittorio Emanuele II 16 | tel. 05 04 22 91 | www.pisaunicaterra.it*

# FOR BOOKWORMS & FILM BUFFS

**Life Is Beautiful (La vita è bella)** – The film (1997) tells the story of a Jewish family from Arezzo in an Italian concentration camp during World War II. Directed by Roberto Benigni (who also plays the lead) it is about a father who tries to distract his young son from the horrors of the war with imaginative stories.

**Inferno** – Film featuring Tom Hanks (2016). While recovering from a period of amnesia, Harvard professor and university sleuth Robert Langdon must embark on another mission to uncover a sinister conspiracy. In the footsteps of Dante, he is chasing a deadly virus through the hidden passages of Florence, trying to prevent the conspirators from letting it loose to eradicate mankind.

**Just one evil act** – Crime novel by Elisabeth George (2014). In another instalment of the Inspector Lynley series, an English girl is kidnapped from a market in Lucca. Delicate, racially and culturally sensitive negotiations ensue.

Vintage for Fans: Iconic Piaggios in the Museum of Pontedera

## WHERE TO GO

### PARCO REGIONALE DI MIGLIARINO, SAN ROSSORE, MASSACIUCCOLI

(144 A–B 5–6, 148 A–B 1–3) *(ℳ D7–9)*
The horses are up for it – they are chomping at their bits, waiting for the starting gates to open. And the gamblers watch with bated breath or loudly cheer on their favourite to win the Palio, the annual horserace of the regional municipalities, which takes place on the former royal country estate Tenuta di San Rossore. The Palio is more than a horserace, it is a country festival. The Tenuta is also a popular starting point for hikes into the nature reserve outside of Pisa where the waters of the swampland among the dark green pine forests reflect the blue sky between the bright yellow reeds.

You can explore it on foot, bicycle, horseback or carriage. The nature park, with its marshy fens, pine avenues, rugged shrubland and the wetlands at the mouth of the river Arno runs all along the coast from Livorno to Viareggio. Another starting point is the guesthouse *La Sterpaia,* where you can get brochures and park products. The signposted *entrance to the park (summer daily 8am–7.30pm, winter 8am–5.30pm | free admission)* at the end of the Viale delle Cascine can be reached from the Via Aurelia North (SS 1). Most of the park area is only accessible by guided tour (fee). Information and reservations in the visitors' centre *Centro Visite San Rossore (Cascine Vecchie | tel. 0 50 53 01 01 | www.parcosanrossore.org).*

### MUSEO PIAGGIO ● (149 D2) *(ℳ F8)*

Since 1946, the iconic scooter Vespa has been produced in Pontedera, 25 km/15.5 mi east of Pisa. In the *factory museum (Tue–Fri 10am–6pm, Sat 10am–1pm and 2–6pm | free admission | Viale Rinaldo Piaggio 7 | www.museopiaggio.it),* you can see "the wasp's" development through the years. Fancy a ride yourself? You can book a tour (from 80 euros, minimum 2 participants), either as a driver or a passenger, at *Agenzia Viaggi Il Fiocco Rosso (Via Bertelli 3 | tel. 05 87 29 10 39 | www.fioccorossoviaggi.it)*

# DISCOVERY TOURS

## ① TUSCANY AT A GLANCE

**START:** ① Pisa
**END:** ⑳ Livorno

10 days
Driving time
(without stops)
14–24 hours

**Distance:**
🚗 approx. 940 km/584 miles

**COSTS:** 1500–2500 euros/2 people (petrol, accommodation, food, admission fees)
**WHAT TO PACK:** swimwear

**IMPORTANT TIPS:** private vehicles are usually prohibited from entering inner cities; keep a look out for parking spaces as soon as you enter the city.
Many of the churches are closed at midday.
You need to reserve tickets in advance to visit the frescoes from Piero della Francesca in ⑫ **Arezzo:** *www.pierodellafrancesca-ticketoffice.it*

Would you like to explore the places that are unique to this region? Then the Discovery Tours are just the thing for you – they include terrific tips for stops worth making, breathtaking places to visit, selected restaurants and fun activities. It's even easier with the Touring App: download the tour with map and route to your smartphone using the QR Code on pages 2/3 or from the website address in the footer below – and you'll never get lost again even when you're offline.

TOURING APP

→ p. 2/3

Magnificent art, delightful bathing resorts, land of plenty and of natural beauty – almost every corner of Tuscany offers all these things. It is virtually impossible to recommend one "perfect" route, but we have tried all the same – knowing all too well that we could have included countless other destinations.

Start your varied tour with a heavy dose of culture in ❶ Pisa → p. 96 on the "field of miracles" around the famous leaning tower and in the medieval old town. After a delicious break, for instance in the **Pasticceria Salza**, there will still be time for the trip to

**DAY 1**

❶ Pisa

24 km/15 mi

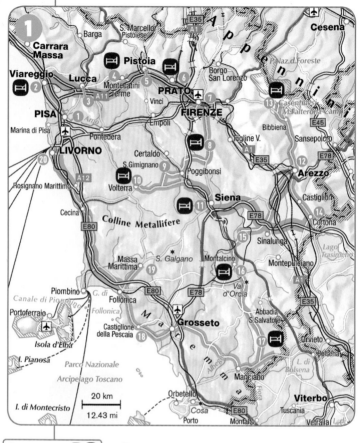

| ② Viareggio | 🚶 🛏 |

**② Viareggio** → p. 96, to enjoy the sunset on the beautiful seaside promenade.

**DAY 2**

| | 31 km/19 mi |
| ③ Lucca | 🍴 🌿 |

| | 33 km/20.5 mi |
| ④ Montecatini | 🅿 🛏 |

A short stretch of motorway separates Viareggio from **③ Lucca** → p. 84 and you should plan half a day to get an impression of this amiable town. You will have a fantastic view from the **Torre Guinigi** platform on the Via Sant'Andrea where the town and its surroundings lie at your feet. **In the afternoon, head to the elegant ④ Montecatini** → p. 46 with its magnificent spa gardens and thermal baths, especially the **Stabilimento Tettuccio**. Here you will be treated to a touch of the belle époque!

The next day explores two cities that undeservedly live in the shadow of Florence. The first is **5 Pistoia** → p. 43, where a stroll through the beautiful old town with its plenty of shops is a must and then – after a light lunch in **I Salaioli** – the textile city **6 Prato** → p. 48, a gem of a city waiting to be discovered behind its ancient walls. Finish your day in the comfortable **La Limonaia**.

Schedule a full day to discover **7 Florence** → p. 32. Once you have visited all the obligatory cultural highlights, you will still have time to stroll through the streets and soak up the city's atmosphere. Take a peek into the artisan and craftsmen workshops around Santo Spirito and Santa Croce; without their skills and craftsmanship, this city on the banks of the River Arno would not enjoy the prosperity and wealth it does today. **In the evening head towards 8 Greve in Chianti** → p. 66. **Shortly before reaching the town on the SR 222 at km 18.5,** you will spot the cosy *agriturismo* **Corte di Valle** *(16 rooms | tel. 05 58 53 9 39 | www.cortedivalle.it | Budget)*, where saffron is grown.

Almost any place in the Chianti region between Florence and Siena is worth a stop but do not succumb to temptation all too often; the magnificent medieval **9 San Gimignano** → p. 68 awaits you **on the other side of the Florence-Siena motorway** as well as the Etruscan town of **10 Volterra** → p. 69 built on porous volcanic rock with the world-famous "Shadow of the Night" sculpture.

It is now on to the next stop at **11 Siena** → p. 60, a red-brick and stone medieval labyrinth of alleyways, where you should definitely spend the whole day. And do not miss out on the delicious local specialties at **Antica Pizzicheria al Palazzo della Chigiana** before you leave!

**Just over 90 km / 56 mi away is 12 Arezzo** → p. 52 where you can visit the famous frescoes of Piero della Francesca and bask in culture as you sit at a restaurant table on the Piazza Grande with its wonderful flair. Then continue along the **lush high valley of Casentino to 13 Poppi** → p. 59. The **I Tre Baroni** resort *(24 rooms | Via di Camaldoli 52 | tel. 05 75 55 62 04 | www.itrebaroni.it | Budget–Expensive)* is your retreat for the evening which offers views towards tomorrow's destination: the medieval fairy tale castle in Poppi.

**DAY 3**
16 km/10 mi
**5 Pistoia**
23 km/14 mi
**6 Prato**

**DAY 4**
24 km/15 mi
**7 Florence**

33 km/20.5 mi

**8 Greve in Chianti**

**DAY 5**
45 km/28 mi
**9 San Gimignano**
30 km/18.5 mi
**10 Volterra**

**DAY 6**
52 km/32 mi
**11 Siena**

**DAY 7**
90 km/56 mi
**12 Arezzo**
38 km/23.5 mi
**13 Poppi**

**DAY 8**

88 km/54.5 mi

⑭ Cortona 🏙

58 km/36 mi

⑮ Monte Oliveto Maggiore 🏠

22 km/13.5 mi

⑯ Montalcino 🏵 🍽

**DAY 9**

72 km/45 mi

⑰ Sorano, Sovana and Pitigliano 🏙 🏠 🏊 🍽

**DAY 10**

127 km/79 mi

⑱ Castiglione della Pescaia 🏙 🎡 🏊

44 km/27 mi

⑲ Massa Marittima 🏙 🏛

108 km/67 mi

⑳ Livorno 🏙

After a walk around the castle, the small Etruscan town of ⑭ **Cortona → p. 58** offers the perfect spot for a relaxed lunch break. **Then take the road via Asciano right through the hilly, lyrical landscape of Crete.** The massive abbey ⑮ **Monte Oliveto Maggiore → p. 65** is well worth a visit. Your destination for today is the wine producing town of ⑯ **Montalcino → p. 66**, where the smells of Brunello accompany you everywhere you go.

Visit the heart of the Etruscan origins in the villages ⑰ **Sorano, Sovana and Pitigliano → p. 78/79**. One artisan inspired by Etruscan art is the goldsmith Silvia Lombardelli at her workshop **Arte Etrusca** *(Via Duomo 24)* in Sovana. In the evening relax at the **INSIDER TIP** Biopool from *agriturismo* **Sant'Egle** *(6 rooms | Via di Case Sparse Sant'Egle 18 | tel. 34 88 88 48 10 | agriturismobiologicotoscana.it | Moderate)* **near Sorano.**

**Today's stretch takes you to the Maremma coast** with the magical ⑱ **Castiglione della Pescaia → p. 74.** After a stroll around the town, enjoy an ice cream sitting at the port and, if the weather permits, a dip in the sea at one of the free beaches on the other side of the port bridge. Your afternoon agenda takes in the medieval work of art ⑲ **Massa Marittima → p. 75** where you will also catch a glimpse of the sea in the distance while you stroll through the town. **The last stage which takes just 108 km / 67 mi is to** ⑳ **Livorno → p. 79**, a port city revealing the more modern face of Tuscany.

## ② ON THE TRAIL OF PIERO DELLA FRANCESCA

| | |
|---|---|
| **START:** ❶ Arezzo<br>**END:** ❶ Arezzo | 8 hours<br>Driving time<br>(without stops)<br>2 hours |
| **Distance:**<br>🚗 85 km/53 miles | |

**COSTS:** admission to the frescoes ❶ Arezzo 8 euros, the museum in ❷ Monterchi 6.50 euros, the museum in ❸ Sansepolcro 10 euros

**IMPORTANT TIPS:** you need to reserve tickets in advance to visit the frescoes from Piero della Francesca in ❶ Arezzo: *www.pierodella francesca-ticketoffice.it*

Painting was his vocation yet mathematics was his true passion: the Tuscan Piero della Francesca (1420–1492) attached great importance to the strict geometric structure of his paintings as well as to the natural representation of his figures, landscapes and light. This approach revolutionised art. Some of his important works are in Arezzo, in his hometown Sansepolcro and in Monterchi, the birthplace of his mother.

**Start in ❶ Arezzo → p. 52. Park your vehicle at the car park at Via Pietri 37 and take the escalator up to the** cathedral → p. 54. In the nave on the left next to the door to the sacristy, his elegant and graceful Maria Magdalena looks down on you from above.

**From the cathedral it is just 500 m / 547 yds to the San Francesco Basilica** → p. 54 where the artist created one

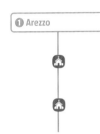

❶ Arezzo

It took Piero della Francesca an entire decade to paint the frescoes in San Francesco

of the most beautiful frescoes in European art history, the ten part series "Legend of the Holy Cross". He spent almost a decade working on the 300 m² / 358 yd² fresco and changed the setting from the Holy Land to Tuscany and into his own time: Arezzo became Jerusalem, the Tuscan countryside became the biblical fields and the Queen of Sheba became a Renaissance noblewoman.

31 km / 19 mi

**❷ Monterchi**

The next stop is the village of ❷ **Monterchi** with the painting of the Madonna del Parto. **Take the SS 73 on the way out of Arezzo towards Sansepolcro. Shortly after the four-lane section of the road comes to an end, the road in Le Ville turns to the right and leads to the village which is then a further 3 km / 1.8 mile away. On a hill below the medieval village centre a brown signpost on the right points the way to the** museum *(April–Oct daily 9am–1pm and 2–7pm, Nov–March 9.30am–12.30pm and 2–5pm | Via Reglia 1)* at the city wall. It was built especially to house the Madonna, a painting that depicts her flanked by two guardian angels and which seems to show the Tuscan peasant country life. It was originally located in the cemetery chapel on the town's outskirts and women prayed in front of it to become pregnant. It was the first time ever that the Madonna was depicted as a pregnant woman. "Immoral!" cried the church that believed Mary always had to be depicted as an immortal virgin and not as an earthly being. It is assumed this is the reason why one of the most brilliant artists of the early Renaissance was literally forgotten about until the 20th century.

15 km / 9.3 mi

From the rear windows of the museum you can look out over exactly the same landscape with its rows of cypress trees, hamlets and rivers that are regular features in

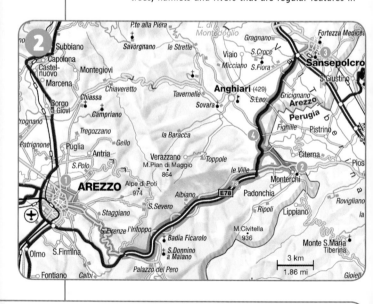

Francesca's paintings. If you arrive in Monterchi at lunchtime, you can spend the time until the museum opens in the afternoon enjoying traditional Tuscan cuisine at the **Vecchia Osteria** *(Closed Tue | Via dell'Ospedale 16 | tel. 0 57 57 01 21 | Moderate)* **on the left above the museum**.

The last stop is ❸ **Sansepolcro** → p. 59, Piero della Francesca's birthplace. **At the northern outskirts of Monterchi take a right turn and follow the SS 73 keeping an eye out for the signpost "Centro" after the motorway bridge. There is free parking at the tree-lined Viale Armando Diaz. In front of the city wall go left up to the Via Aggiunti and turn right. The town's museum is at no. 65,** the **Museo Civico Sansepolcro** *(mid-June–mid-Sept daily 10am–1.30pm and 2.30–7pm, mid-Sept–mid-June 10am–1pm and 2.30–6pm | www.museocivicosansepolcro.it)* with four of the artist's paintings: the"La Madonna della Misericordia" and three murals including "La Resurrenzione", said by the writer Aldous Huxley to be the most beautiful Renaissance painting of all. In the fresco the Son of God, marked by death, emerges from his tomb, unnoticed by the guards. The INSIDER TIP diagonal composition gives depth to the background while in the foreground the figures are very vivid because of the artist's clever use of light. If you haven't already eaten in Monterchi, **a few houses further at no. 83** is the highly acclaimed restaurant **Al Coccio** *(Closed Tue | tel. 05 75 74 14 68 | www.alcoccio.com | Moderate).*

**Next to the museum is the town's medieval centre. On the left along the Via della Fonte you will reach the home of the painter.** After a devastating fire, only the stairs and a fountain at the entrance remain of the original building. If you still have some time, walk through the pretty town centre and enjoy the comfortable pace of this small town with its many shops and cosy bars.

Schedule around an hour for the return trip to Arezzo. If you get hungry along the way, stop at ❹ **Locanda al Castello di Sorci** *(Closed Mon | San Lorenzo district 25 | tel. 05 75 78 90 66 | www.castellodisorci.it | Budget–Moderate)* **en route,** where you can choose from a selection of fresh daily specials. **Then return to ❶ Arezzo along the route you came.**

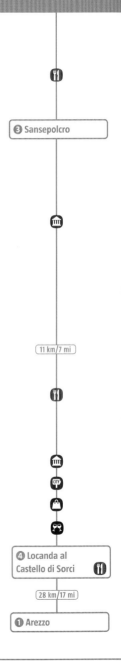

❸ Sansepolcro

11 km/7 mi

❹ Locanda al Castello di Sorci

28 km/17 mi

❶ Arezzo

# ③ HIKING UP MONTE SAGRO IN THE MARBLE MOUNTAINS

| START: ❶ Rifugio Carrara | 1 day |
| END: ❶ Rifugio Carrara | Hiking time (without stops) 4–5 hours |
| Distance: medium difficulty | |
| 🏁 10 km/6 mi ▮▮▮ Height: 500 m/1640 ft | |

**WHAT TO PACK:** sturdy footwear, sun and rain protection, snacks, water bottle, trekking poles if required

**IMPORTANT TIPS:** entrance to car park at the starting point on the SP 59 Carrara–Campo Cecina. Direct ATN bus connection on Sundays in summer at 9.30am (line 39 leaving from the bus station Piazza Sacco e Vanzetti in Carrara, timetable: *www.atnsrl.it*, keyword: Orari Linee Carrara, Linea 39).
Mountaineering experience is advisable as the final section is very steep.

Throughout the world the name Carrara is synonymous with marble, the coveted white stone. Virtually every country in the world has at least one monument or hotel foyer made from the white stone mined in the Apuan Alps since Roman times. Artists such as Michelangelo used material from the north-west of Tuscany for their sculptures. Stretching over just 100 km²/38 mi² and elevated to almost 2000 m/6561 ft, the rocky karst mountains are also a paradise for hikers.

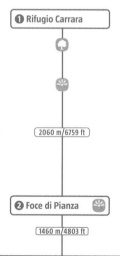

❶ Rifugio Carrara

2060 m/6759 ft

❷ Foce di Pianza

1460 m/4803 ft

The hike sets off at an altitude of 1320 m/4330 ft from the Italian Alpine Club mountain hut ❶ **Rifugio Carrara** *(tel. 05 85 84 19 72)* which is open all year round. **The hiking trail marked 173 first takes you across an alpine meadow past the remains of ancient shepherd dwellings in a shady beech forest. On the northern side of Monte Borla you will reach a boulder field.** Here you can enjoy a picture postcard view of the mountain landscape of Lunigiana in the North dominated by the stone cathedral of Pizzo d'Uccello.

IIn the valley between Monte Borla and Monte Sagro the first stone quarries appear. **Continuing at this altitude in a southerly direction you will reach the pass ❷ Foce di Pianza** (1289 m/4229 ft) where a marble road is used by trucks to transport the heavy blocks into the valley. You can also drive up to this point by car. At this height, the Gulf of La Spezia and the world's largest marble mining area lie at your feet. In the Carrara hinterland alone there are some 85 quarries in operation and 185 in total in the Apuan Alps. From afar, some of them resemble rock castles, others rocky cubist arenas. Wire ropes were once used to excavate the rock from the mountains requiring sand and water which explains the many rusty tanks that lie around.

**From the Foce di Pianza pass, proceed on hiking trail no. 172, first over a wide ridge and then left along the mountainside.** There you can see some trenches, remnants of the Gothic Line, a defensive line used by the Germans to retreat in World War II. **Half an hour later you will reach the** ❸ **Foce della Faggiola Pass** (1464 m/4803 ft). From up here you look down on the marble village of Colonnata. Although today the village's name is primarily associated with the exquisite fatty bacon that is cured here in marble vats, it was once the place that supplied Michelangelo with his marble.

The aromatic *lardo di Colonnat* matures in marble basins

❸ Foce della Faggiola

1110 m / 3642 ft

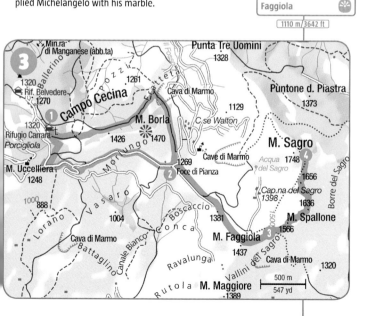

④ Monte Sagro

4750 m / 15,584 ft

❶ Rifugio Carrara

The last leg to the summit of ④ **Monte Sagro** at **1750 m / 5741 ft** is marked in blue. **The route first takes you across a treeless hillside meadow; behind the north-west side it becomes steeper.** As a reward you will be able to see from the viewing platform, to the West the sea and to the East the endless vistas of cliffs and forest, with small alpine villages dotted here and there. The village directly below is Vinca where German SS soldiers staged a revenge campaign in 1944.

**The return trip is the same way as far as the Pianza Pass. Instead of walking right back through the beech forest to the mountain hut, you can walk approx. 2 km / 1.2 mile on the broad marble road. Then a narrow forest trail turns off to the right that takes you back to** ❶ **Rifugio Carrara** where you can fill up on *panini* and pasta. From its panoramic terrace you can see Corsica on a clear day.

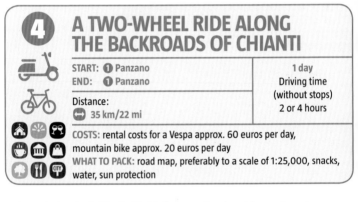

# 4  A TWO-WHEEL RIDE ALONG THE BACKROADS OF CHIANTI

| START: ❶ Panzano<br>END: ❶ Panzano | 1 day<br>Driving time<br>(without stops)<br>2 or 4 hours |
|---|---|
| Distance:<br>🚲 35 km/22 mi | |

**COSTS:** rental costs for a Vespa approx. 60 euros per day, mountain bike approx. 20 euros per day
**WHAT TO PACK:** road map, preferably to a scale of 1:25,000, snacks, water, sun protection

For centuries *strade bianche* ("white" or unsurfaced roads) were the only means of connecting remote villages and wine estates. They led over hills and were flanked by cypress trees so that people could see them from afar. This tour from Panzano to the wine estate Castello di Volpaia and to Radda in Chianti is a highlight for those who love scenic landscapes – and on a Vespa or mountain bike the experience will be far more exhilarating with the play of light on the hills or the smell of the surrounding countryside.

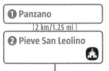

❶ Panzano

[ 2 km/1.25 mi ]

❷ Pieve San Leolino

In ❶ **Panzano, first take a short detour to the little church** ❷ **Pieve San Leolino at the edge of the village. From the Strada Chiantigiana (SR 222) turn left after about 1 km/0.6 mi from the town.** The Romanesque building with its picturesque cloister was a stopover for pilgrims

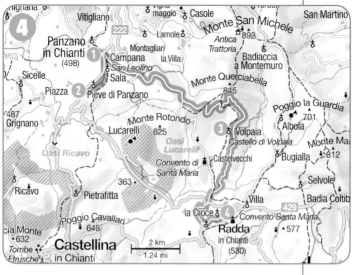

and believers during the Middle Ages. Just before the clois-ter stands the **Villa Le Barone**, an INSIDER TIP aristocratic villa in park surroundings. Take a break for an expresso or cappuccino in the villa bar.

**Stay on the narrow road towards the north until you reach a crossroads where you can turn left to Panzano. Here you take the road to the right to Montemaggio; it turns into a gravel road after a few metres. Now you cannot get lost anymore. Simply follow the white signs to the Castello di Volpaia.** Initially the road is lined with cypresses. The landscape then becomes wilder, the undergrowth thicker and mighty oaks and massive rocks line the way. Alternating to the left and right the hilly landscape opens up and you can see to the horizon on both sides. Chestnut trees alternate with spruce and beeches and during spring, lots of yellow broom.

**At the halfway mark you will find a shady rest area under high trees** where you can pause and soak up the nature around. As soon as the cypresses start to become more frequent you are almost at the final destination. **Just after a narrow curve,** the charming roof ensemble of ❸ **Castello di Volpaia** *(tel. 05 77 73 80 66 | www.volpaia.*

10 km/6 mi

❸ Castello di Volpaia

The most authentic experience in Chianti along the unpaved *strade bianche*

6 km/3.7 mi

**4** Radda in Chianti

16 km/10 mi

**1** Panzano

*com)* appears in the distance. It is a fortified wine estate that dates back to the 11th century and the owners have carefully restored the almost perfectly preserved medieval castle village and given it a new life.

On the tiny village square Paola Barucci conjures up delicious panini with Tuscan specialties in **Bar Ucci** *(Closed Mon | www.bar-ucci.it)* and in the *enoteca (May–Oct Thu–Tue 10.30am–6.30pm)* next door you can buy wine and olive oil from the estate. **A paved road leads from the village square further on to 4 Radda in Chianti → p. 66** and thus back to the present day. Take a stroll through the centre and enjoy a drink before **heading back along the same road to 1 Panzano.**

## 5 TO THE HEART OF ETRUSCAN CULTURE AND SEASIDE AT MAREMMA

| | |
|---|---|
| **START:** 1 Grosseto<br>**END:** 6 Castiglione della Pescaia | **1 day**<br>Driving time<br>(without stops)<br>a good 2 hours |
| **Distance:**<br>→ a good 80 km/50 mi | |

**COSTS:** approx. 30 euros/2 people (petrol, car park costs, museum admission fees)
**WHAT TO PACK:** swimwear

Spurred on by the abundance of mineral resources in a region once covered in marshland, the south west of Tuscany has witnessed a constant stream of rulers over the last two millennia. However the true lords of Maremma were in fact the Etruscans. They were the first to drain the marshes, mine iron ore and build flourishing settlements and impressive necropolises.

This is why you should start this tour in ❶ Grosseto → p. 70 in the archeological museum in the heart of the historic town centre. It offers a vivid documentation of the Etruscan period in Maremma. To visit the town, leave your car outside the city walls at one of the many parking spaces available – except on market day on Thursday mornings. For a provincial town, the museum is surprisingly large with 40 rooms spread over three floors and boasts well maintained statues, ornaments and ceramics such as the *ciotola di bucchero* bowl from the 6th century BC engraved with Etruscan writing.

Many of the artefacts were found in the Etruscan town of ❷ Roselle, accessible from Grosseto along the main road to Siena. There is nothing left here today to remind visitors that the town was once a powerful city state two and a half millennia ago. However at the well signposted archaeological excavation site, Rusellae *(daily 8.30am– sunset)* you can walk around the remains of Etruscan houses, workshops and public buildings and through the Roman amphitheatre built somewhat later where con-

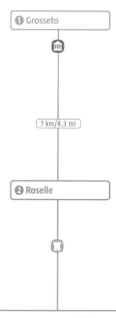

❶ Grosseto

🏛

7 km/4.3 mi

❷ Roselle

🏰

certs and theatre performances are organised today on summer evenings.

26 km/16 mi

Its old rival Vetulonia stands here in view. This was once the most powerful Etruscan city state and was founded on the banks of Lago Prile, a large salt lake which until the 7th century BC covered the entire flatland of Grosseto. **Now take the SP 41 to Castiglione della Pescaia.** You will drive past the vineyard **Mustiaio** *(www.mustiaio.it)*, where you can pick up a few bottles of Vermentino and past the **fruit and vegetable stand run by the farmer Orlando** which is open all year round.

**At the end of the road turn left and, directly after the bridge along the SS 1 turn right to Buriano and then right again at the end.** After approx. 3 km / 1.8 mi you will spot the roadside trattoria and bar ❸ **Il Bozzone** *(in the winter closed Tue | Budget),* a type of modern-day post office where farmers from neighbouring villages, passing truckers, tourists looking to buy provisions for their evening meal and hunters spinning yarns all come together. The INSIDER TIP daily menu serving authentic food from Maremma is both tasty and affordable.

❸ Il Bozzone

11 km/7 mi

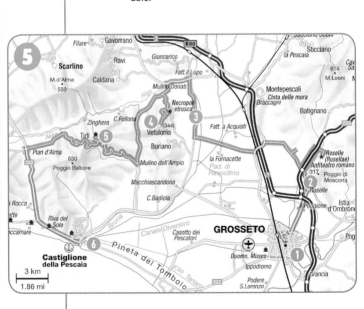

Arrived! Castiglione is the most picturesque seaside resort in Tuscany

Your next destination is Grilli from where you take a left up to ❹ **Vetulonia**, as it is known today. **The most important excavation sites are located at the entrance to the village:** although slightly neglected in appearance, the remains of Etruscan settlements and necropolises can be visited here free of charge. It's also worth taking a look in the museum in the village where the burial objects are kept.

A spot of sea breeze is surely what you need after this heavy dose of Etruscan culture! **To head for the coast, take the Strada Provinciale Strette down in Grilli through delightful olive groves and forests to Castiglione della Pescaia. After 10 km / 6 mi turn right up to ❺ Tirli**, a small mountain village with the excellent restaurant Il Cacciatore *(In the winter closed Tue | Piazza del Popolo 15 | tel. 05 64 94 58 20 | Moderate)*, **and from there back down to the SP 158 coastal road.**

**Take a left at the crossroads in Pian d'Alma to reach ❻ Castiglione della Pescaia → p. 74.** At the most picturesque seaside resort in the whole of Tuscany, a day's hire of one parasol and two sun loungers will cost you 35 euros at the beach promenade. Spend the day instead at one of the free beaches at the entrance to the resort or after the harbour bridge on the road to Marina di Grosseto. **The best place to park your car is on the left in the pine grove. Then cross the road and look for the path down to the beach between the houses.** During the day you may have to share some sections of the beach with kite surfers yet stay until sunset to enjoy the beach virtually to yourself.

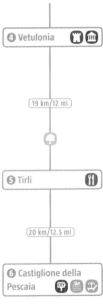

❹ Vetulonia

19 km / 12 mi

❺ Tirli

20 km / 12.5 mi

❻ Castiglione della Pescaia

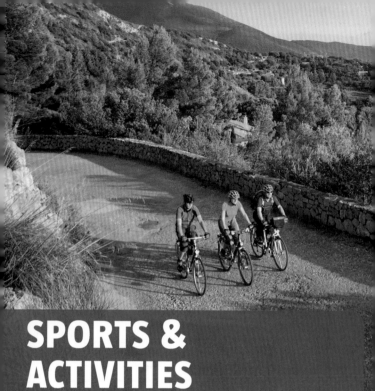

# SPORTS & ACTIVITIES

**In Tuscany many people are devoted to sport and visiting holidaymakers also benefit from the extensive leisure activities on offer. An active holiday is the ideal accompaniment to pasta, wine and culture.**

## CYCLING

Cycling is a favourite sport in the region. During weekends, there are throngs of cyclists on the roads and as the conditions are often hilly and steep with winding country tracks, they are also ideal for the more ambitious cyclists. The same goes for mountain bikers that can often be seen on the high plateaus of the Apuan Alps, the Apennines or on Monte Amiata, not always to the delight of conservationists. Many communities have responded to the growing demand and offer cycling-themed packages on their websites. The province of Siena and Mugello are especially active. See *www. terresiena.it* and *www.mugellotoscana.it* for information about bicycle rentals and cyclist-friendly accommodation. A curiosity is the historic cycling race *Eroica (www. eroica-ciclismo.it)* during the autumn in Chianti. Anyone can participate – provided that there is still a place left – and provided that you use a bicycle that is more than 20 years old and dress in clothing from yesteryear.

## HIKING

Tuscany is Italy's most densely wooded region and has exceptional trails, even

Photo: Monte Argentario

In Tuscany you can be sporty – on a bicycle or on horseback – or relax in the spas and thermal baths of the health resorts

by Europe's high standards. It is not surprising then that it is covered in a dense network of themed trails – e.g. in the footsteps of St Francis of Assisi – that are generally well maintained and clearly marked. The most famous pilgrim route running from France to Rome, the *Via Francigena (www. viefrancigene.org),* also has a dozen stages that pass through Tuscany; the website provides detailed maps and an extensive list of addresses. The ideal hiking time is from mid-April to mid-June and then again in September and October. On weekends you will be sharing the trails with the many Italians who by now love hiking as much as their northern neighbours. During the week, however, you may often have the trails all to yourself. Many routes have holiday farms, bed & breakfast or eco-accommodation along the way. In almost every Pro Loco tourist information office you can get free detailed maps and on the website at *www. turismo.intoscana.it* (choose the English language option and the "trekking" in the search tab). There is also a *Walking Festival (www.tuscanywalkingfestival.it)* with many events organised throughout the region from mid-April to November.

the horses and organise meals and accommodation. The *Turismo Equestro* ensures high standards and is marked by the symbol of a white compass rose against a red background with a green

To Elba for a spot of lunch? No problem for a sailor!

## HORSEBACK RIDING

The Maremma region is well known as a riding paradise, the appropriate infrastructure is in place because traditionally the cattle in the Maremma nature reserve are herded on horseback and experienced riders can accompany the Tuscan cowboys, the *butteri*, by appointment: *Azienda Agricola Alberese (www.alberese.com)*. But there are also plenty of other areas of untouched nature such as in Garfagnana, in Casentino or in the Orcia Valley where there are *ippovie* – horse trails – scenic routes. In many places holiday farms such as the horse riding centre *Vallebona (www.vallebona.it)* near Pontassieve offer multi-day riding treks. They provide

horse's head. The best addresses for riding holidays in Tuscany can be found (only in Italian) at *www.turismoequestre. com* (search term "Toscana").

## MEDITATION & YOGA

Tuscany's rolling hills and deep forests are the ideal place for weary souls to kick back and leave the daily grind far behind. A number of "agriturismi" offer yoga, mindfulness and meditation classes and the nature parks organise courses and themed weeks. Many ancient monasteries and hermitages now offer spiritual retreats - we recommend the hermitage of Camaldoli and the Order of the Vallombrosans. www.bookyogaretreats. com offers three- to eight-day courses, hiking included in some of them. Whether you prefer the countryside or the seaside, country-style or with bells and whistles, Tuscany truly caters to all tastes.

## ROCK CLIMBING

Relatively undiscovered outside the local climbing community, Tuscany is in fact a fantastic destination for climbers. With over 40 different rock climbing areas to choose from (not including the island of Elba), you could find yourself alone on the rock face if you're there during the week. The range of rock climbing available is varied from closed down quarries, hidden tufa rocks in dense forests to craggy limestone cliffs. And there is something for everyone: climbing parks for those who prefer a safe and comfortable climb as well as more demanding routes and ascents where advanced climbers can test their skills. Many of the sites are situated in the Apuan Alps above Versilia, near Massa and Carrara. The red limestone cliffs near Monsummano in Apennin and the conglomerate rock crags near San Vivaldo are also extremely popular. Most areas offer climbing schools with professional climbing instructors.

## WATER SPORTS

Along the coast, water sports fans have an endless array of possibilities. Boat owners can drop anchor in one of the various large or small ports as well as in the natural bays. There are ideal conditions for scuba divers on the rocky Monte Argentario coast, in front of the Piombino foothills or along the coast south of Livorno. There are dive centres in Porto Santo Stefano, Piombino and Livorno. The wind along the coast of the Tyrrhenian Sea is also perfect for wind-

surfers and sailors. Apart from courses you can book a sailing trip with a skipper to the whale sanctuary Pelagos in the island archipelago. Information: *www. costadeglietruschi.it,* tab: *sport and recreation* then *sail and windsurf.*

## WELLNESS & SPAS

Thermal water to treat the body and soul was something that even the Romans enjoyed in Tuscany. Two thousand years later during the 18th century these ancient thermal baths were transformed into noble spa resorts like *Bagni di Lucca* or the spa of *Montecatini Terme* where the rich and powerful took refuge to treat rheumatism, reduce their blood pressure, clear their lungs or simply rejuvenate. These spas have developed into a veritable wellness industry over the past years; the curative water spa *Equi Terme* in the Apuan Alps, the natural caves of *Grotta Giusti* near Pisa, the outdoor sources of Bagni di Petriolo, the luxurious thermal waters in San Casciano dei Bagni on the border to Latium and the classic *Chianciano Terme* where purifying herbal drinking cures are served to rejuvenate tired bodies are just to name a few. In the town of Saturnia in the south of Tuscany warm water at 37 °C gushes from natural pools. Visitors however are greeted with the stench of rotting eggs caused by the sulphates in the mineral salts. Numerous private beauty spas have literally sprung up around the resort, offering the entire range of wellness treatments, some in remote sites like the *Villa Ferraia* near Monticiano and others in town centres like the Golden Tower Spa Hotel in Florence.

You can find information on the complete range of offers available at *www. turismo.intoscana.it/en;* search term Wellness.

# TRAVEL WITH KIDS

Children love a beach holiday and Tuscany, with its long sandy beaches and shady pine groves, is perfect. On the coast here are numerous blue flag beaches while in the interior there are medieval villages behind every hill that could have come straight out of the Inkheart series or the Twilight saga. The holiday farms are the cherry on top.

## FLORENCE & THE NORTH

### MUSEO CON PERSONAGGI IN MOVIMENTO IN SCARPERIA
(147 D3) (*∅ K6*)

Tinkers, basket weavers and cheese makers are only three of the 65 movable wooden figures that demonstrate everyday life in a typical Mugello village during the first half of the 20th century. The museum's creator, Falerio Lepri, shows his little works of art on *Sundays (summer 3.30pm–6.30pm, winter 3pm–6pm)* and by appointment. *District Sant'Agata | Via Montaccianico | tel. 05 58 40 67 50*

### MUSEO STIBBERT IN FLORENCE ●
(146 C5) (*∅ J–K7*)

A chamber of wonders! In the 19th century the eccentric Englishman, Frederick Stibbert, filled his massive villa with souvenirs and unusual objects from around the world. The fairy tale castle is situated in a beautiful park and is easily reached with the no. 4 bus from the train station. *Museum Mon–Wed 10am–2pm, Fri–Sun 10am–6pm, guided tour every hour on the*

Photo: Giardino dei Tarocchi

Lots of room for fun and games: kids young and old can get the most out of Tuscany

hour, park daily 8am–7pm, winter until 5pm | museum 8 euros, children under 6 years 6 euros, free admission to park | Via Federigo Stibbert 26 | www.museo stibbert.it

### PARCO AVVENTURA IL GIGANTE
### IN VAGLIA (144 C4) (*∅ J6–7*)
Skate, climb or swing through trees on seven different courses in this adventure park. Three hours of fun are guaranteed, every extra hour is 5 euros. Helmet and climbing harness included in the price.

June–Sept daily 10am–7.30pm, May Mon– Fri 2–7pm, Sat / Sun 10am–7pm, April and Oct Sat/Sun 10am–6.30pm | 18 euros, children 12–15 euros depending on age | Via Fiorentina 276 | www.parcoaventura ilgigante.it

### PARCO DI PINOCCHIO IN COLLODI
(145 D4) (*∅ F7*)
A whisper path, a fairy cloud and a Venetian lagoon carousel: the theme park in the home town of Pinocchio's inventor Carlo Lorenzini is full of surprises. In the wonder-

ful baroque gardens of the *Villa Garzoni* next door is butterfly house. *March–Oct daily 9am–sunset, Nov–Feb 10am–sunset | combi ticket 22 euros (in winter 18 euros), reduction for children and over 65 | Via San Gennaro 3 | www.pinocchio.it*

### PARCO DEI MOSTRI IN BOMARZO
(0) (*P–Q18*)

Just beyond Tuscany near Viterbo in the Latium region, there is a park full of frightening monsters and bizarre sights you absolutely must see. For 450 years, moth-

The colourful markets attract young fashionistas

## AREZZO, SIENA & CHIANTI

### ACCADEMIA DEI FISIOCRITICI IN SIENA
(151 D6) (*K11*)

Full to the brim with curiosities collected over three hundred years of scientific history, this Natural History Museum excites young explorers with ceramic mushrooms for teaching purposes or water specimens extracted from Tuscan thermal springs. The building, previously a Camaldolese monastery, houses two centuries of acquisitions and donations. The skeleton of a 15-metre fin whale welcomes you in the courtyard. Ring the doorbell! *Mon–Fri 9am–2pm | free admission | Piazzetta Silvio Gigli 2 | www. fisiocritici.it*

er nature has had her way with the monsters of Bomarzo and the place is simply magical. Ideal for a picnic or a barbecue. Leave the A 1 at Attigliano or come via Viterbo and take the Via del Lavatoio, passing Bomarzo in the North. *April–Aug daily 8.30am–7pm, Sept–March 8.30am– sunset | 10 euros, children (4–13 years) 8 euros | www.parcodeimostri.com*

## MAREMMA & COSTA DEGLI ETRUSCHI

### ACQUA VILLAGE IN CECINA MARE
(148 C6) (*E11*)

Giant slides, Jacuzzi lagoon, wave pool, beach volleyball and a baby club: holiday fun is guaranteed. Almost

60 km / 37 mi to the south in Follonica, district Mezzaluna is a second water park with similar facilities. *Mid-June–mid-Sept daily 10am–6pm / 25 euros, after 2.30pm 19 euros, children (3–11 years) 19 euros, after 2.30pm 14 euros, reductions during low season | Via Tevere 25 | www.acquavillage.it*

### CAVALLINO MATTO IN MARINA DI CASTAGNETO ⊛ (154 A2) (*ⱴ E12*)

An ecologically sustainable fun park with miniature railways, mini golf and jumping castles for the little ones and roller coaster, white water route and quad bike trail for the older ones, they also have a nature and eco-trail. *April–May mostly Thu–Sun 10am–6pm, June Thu–Tue 10am–6pm, July–1st half of Sept daily 10.30am–6.30pm | 24 euros, children under 130 cm / 51 inches 17 euros, under 100 cm / 39 inches free, after 2.30pm adults and children 14 euros | Via Po 1 | www.cavallinomatto.it*

### IL GIARDINO DEI TAROCCHI (159 E4) (*ⱴ L18*)

The larger than life, colourful objects are not just for looking at. Children are allowed to peek inside or climb on top. *April–mid-Oct daily 2.30–7.30pm, Nov–March 1st Sat of the month 9am–1pm | 12 euros, children (7–18 years) 7 euros, Nov–March free | www.nikidesaintphalle.com*

### INSIDER TIP ▶ PARCO ARCHEO-MINERARIO DI SAN SILVESTRO (154 B3) (*ⱴ F13*)

Visitors can today go on a discovery into the mountain mining history of the Colline Metallifere, where the Etruscan got their riches from centuries ago. This includes a visit the mining museum and a trip on the small yellow train in a disused tunnel. *March–May and Oct Sat / Sun 10am–6pm, June and Sept Tue–Sun 10am–7pm, July / Aug daily 9.30am–7.30pm | 16 euros with guided tour, children (6–14 years) 12 euros | www.parchivaldicornia.it*

### PARCO AVVENTURA CIELO VERDE IN MARINA DI GROSSETO (158 A1) (*ⱴ H16*)

Long, wide beaches, easy cycle paths and clean water are exactly why this coastal suburb of Grosseto got the "child-friendly" label. It is also no coincidence that the Florentine adventure park, Il Gigante, has a branch in the camping village Cieloverde during summer. *Mid-June–mid-Sept daily 10am–7pm | 2½ hours 18 euros, children (7–12 years) 15 euros, 3–6 years 10 euros, every additional hour 5 euros | Via della Trappola 180 | www.parcoavventura cieloverde.it*

## LUCA, PISA & VERSILIA

### GROTTA DEL VENTO NEAR FORNOVOLASCO (143 E5) (*ⱴ D5–6*)

Stalactites, stalagmites, underground streams and lakes: discovered in the caves in the Apuan Alps on three comfortable and well-lit circular paths. *Daily 10am–6pm on the hour (except 1pm) | depending on the tour 9/14/20 euros, children under 10 years 7/11/16 euros | www.grottadelvento.com*

### PARCO AVVENTURA IN FOSDINOVO (142 C4) (*ⱴ B5*)

6 aerial obstacle courses with 50 obstacles promise adventure for everyone: mountain bike course, archery range, a range for mini quads, bungee trampoline, swaying rope bridges and exciting 200 m of zip wires. *Varying opening hours, please refer to the website, mostly weekends | 21 euros, youth 16 euros, children 9 euros | Via Cucco | www.parcoavventura fosdinovo.com*

# FESTIVALS & EVENTS

Tuscans love to celebrate and there are festivals or tournaments for every occasion: a patron saint, a pagan custom, or an event in the city's history. A good option is a ● **INSIDER TIP** *sagra*, a local festival serving specialities.

## EVENTS & FESTIVALS

### FEBRUARY/MARCH

Highlight of the *carnival* are the allegorical papier mâché figures in Viareggio that are dragged along the seaside promenade.

### GOOD FRIDAY

The *Venerdì Santo* of Grassina (suburb of Florence) is the Tuscan version of a Passion play.

### APRIL–MID-JUNE

At the end of April the *Maggio Musicale Fiorentino,* the oldest music festival for modern classical music, starts in Florence.

### MAY

Eight boats with twelve crew are racing 600 metres (656 yds) towards a 12-metre (40 ft)pole to snatch a flag at the *Giostra dell'Antenna* in Livorno's oldest rowing tradition going back to Medieval times. It takes place on the closest Sunday to the 21st of May.

On the last two Sundays of May, Lucignano near Arezzo celebrates spring with a colourful **INSIDER TIP** *flower carnival Maggiolata.*

### JUNE

On the 17th of June, in Pisa is the *Regata di San Ranieri,* a race with historic rowing boats on the Arno River, and on the last Sunday in June, the *Gioco del Ponte:* on the Arno bridge Ponte di Mezzo, muscled men push a heavy trolley to the opposite side of the bridge.

At the *Calcio Storico Fiorentino* in Florence on the 24th of June, three teams fight over a cloth ball. The day ends with a fireworks display.

### JULY/AUGUST

The *Palio* in Siena (2 July, 16 Aug): ten riders on unsaddled horses race three times around the Piazza del Campo (it's over in about 100 seconds).

At the blues festival *Pistoia Blues* in July on the cathedral square, legends like B.B. King or the Talking Heads have played.

*La Versiliana,* the multi-genre festival in Pietrasanta, is a meeting point for tourists who want a dash of culture.

## Sports, games, food, medieval tournaments or jazz concerts: Tuscan events come in many forms

***Effetto Venezia*** is a nine day carnival/ funfair at the end of July/early August in Livorno with music, dance, cabaret and folklore.

***Grey Cat Jazz Festival:*** You can hear the best international and Italian acts everywhere in the province of Grosseto, usually in August. Ticket prices vary concert to concert.

The historic game ***Bravio delle Botti*** on the last Sunday of August draws many visitors to Montepulciano. Wine barrels are rolled up the steep streets to the Piazza Grande. An exciting competition between the eight districts fo the town.

### SEPTEMBER

The ***Giostra del Saracino*** in Arezzo (1st Sun) is a colourful costume festival, where riders have to hit a wooden figure with a lance. Great for fans of the Middle Ages.

Choirs from all over Europe travel to the acclaimed competition ***Concorso Polifonico*** in Arezzo during mid-September.

### END OF OCTOBER

***Lucca Comics & Games:*** the name says it all. Great fun for the whole family on the largest comic festival in Europe.

## NATIONAL HOLIDAYS

| | |
|---|---|
| 1 Jan | *Capodanno* |
| 6 Jan | *Epifania* |
| March/April | Easter Monday (*Pasquetta*) |
| 25 April | *Liberazione* (anniversary of the liberation from German occupation) |
| 1 May | *Festa del Lavoro* |
| 2 June | *Festa della Repubblica* (Republic Day) |
| 15 Aug | *Ferragosto* |
| 1 Nov | *Ognissanti* |
| 8 Dec | *Immacolata Concezione* |
| 25/26 Dec | *Natale/Santo Stefano* |

# LINKS, BLOGS, APPS & MORE

**LINKS & BLOGS**

**www.toscanainfesta.it** This website (only Italian) lists the countless folk festivals that take place all over Tuscany. Many of which celebrate local culinary specialities such as the wild boar or mushroom festivals and there is even a doughnut festival

**www.atlantidephototravel.com** Some excellent landscape photographs by three Florentine photographers to get you in the holiday mood. Simply enter "Tuscany" in the search field

**guaizine.tumblr.com** A visual diary kept by photographer Martin Leon who posts candid shots of events mainly held in Florence on fashion, culture and day-to-day life revealing what's really behind the city's Renaissance facade

**www.tuscanylowcost.com** The name says it all: here you can find cheap holiday homes throughout the region

**www.facebook.com/VisitTuscany** This is where fans of Tuscany can rave about the region, share their experiences and post suggestions for the next trip

**smartexpat.com/italy/florence** This blog is geared to expats living in Tuscany but it is also full of useful tourist tips with an events guide and a classified section

**allafiorentina.com** Krista Ricchi is originally from California, but now lives in Florence and shares her discoveries – especially in the fields of fashion, food, fine art, markets and yoga

**www.toomuchtuscany.com** Beautiful blog about all things Tuscany – from Siena to Chianti, from bike tours to the grape harvest. Tuscany off the beaten track!

**wikitravel.org/en/Talk:Tuscany** Open source travel guide featuring up-to-date information on attractions, hotels, restaurants, travel tips and more.

Regardless of whether you are still researching your trip or already in Tuscany: these addresses will provide you with more information, videos and networks to make your holiday even more enjoyable

en.julskitchen.com Giulia teaches Tuscan cooking classes. On her website, she shares lots of delicious Tuscan recipes with us, invites us to workshops and throws in some tips on travelling in Tuscany, too

www.youtube.com/visittuscany The Tuscan tourism website has an interactive map that allows you to select a village or town and then watch a video or you can choose from a number of different categories such as "Seaside", "Mountainside", "Spa" etc.

**VIDEOS**

www.youtube.com/watch?v=r9C5hutVsPg&feature=related Impressions which capture the atmosphere of a winter walk through San Gimignano

www.youtube.com/watch?v=1mr8Hy6tLYk Final scene from the 1993 Shakespeare movie "Much Ado About Nothing" starring Emma Thompson and Kenneth Branagh: like the entire film, it's full of zest for life – and beautiful Tuscan scenery

**APPS**

Tuscany+ is the augmented reality app for iPhone that was created by the Tuscan Tourism Department (see also www. turismo.intoscana). Load it on to your phone and hold the internal camera on a point, and a map appears with tags with information about sightseeing attractions, hotels and restaurants in the immediate vicinity

IMIBACT Free app for iOS and Android. Find the state museums that interest you with this geolocalized list. Each one has a bit of a description and some images of famous works to help you figure out what artworks are not to miss. Current exhibitions are also listed.

Firenze Turismo You can download this iOS and Android-compatible app for free from the communal *www.firenzeturismo.it/en* (–> *Download our apps)* website to help you find your way around and be best informed about what is happening in the city as well as in its provinces

The Publisher shall not be held responsible for the contents of the links, blogs, apps, etc. listed here

# TRAVEL TIPS

## ARRIVAL

When travelling by car the most comfortable route is to take the Brenner pass and the A 22 to Modena and from there further on the A 1 via Bologna to Florence. If you are travelling via Switzerland, take the A 1 in Milan to Modena, Bologna, Florence. An alternative is the stretch Milan–Parma, from there the A 15 and the Cisa pass to La Spezia and further towards Pisa. The motorways in Italy, Austria and Switzerland charge tolls. You can find the current toll prices at *www. autostrade.it/en/* keyword *tolls.* From July until September trucks are banned from driving on the motorways during weekends.

Trains via Austria arrive in Florence via the Brenner and Bologna. There is a direct night train to Florence from Munich and Vienna, during the day you need to change in Bologna. Trains via Switzerland travel either on the Milan–Genova–Livorno–Grosseto route or the Milan–Bologna–Florence route. From Florence you can travel in any direction on the regional rail lines. Tickets are available at counters or vending machines. You must remember to stamp your ticket in the stamping machines on the train station platform before travelling. *www.nationalrail.co.uk, www.bahn.de, www.oebb. at, www.sbb.ch, www.trenitalia.com*.

Travelling by bus is usually the cheapest, but not really the quickest way to get around. Check out comparison portals like www.goeurope.com or www. checkmybus.com. Many providers in Italy also stop in the smaller towns, for instance Balotour, the Italian subsidiary of Flixbus, or Interbus and Mariano Autolinee.

Pisa's *Aeroporto Galileo Galilei* is the major airport hub in Tuscany and has good international links. From the airport there are regular trains and buses to Pisa's main station and a shuttle goes to Florence several times a day. Florence's airport is connected to the main railway station Santa Maria Novella by bus. If you plan to stay in the southern parts of Tuscany, you could also consider flying to Rome.

## RESPONSIBLE TRAVEL

It doesn't take a lot to be environmentally friendly whilst travelling. Don't just think about your carbon footprint whilst flying to and from your holiday destination but also about how you can protect nature and culture abroad. As a tourist it is especially important to respect nature, look out for local products, cycle instead of driving, save water and much more. If you would like to find out more about eco-tourism please visit: *www.ecotourism.org*

## ACCOMMODATION

### AGRITURISMO
Hundreds of farms in Tuscany have guest rooms and apartments available for tourists. They range from simple rooms to suites on wine estates. They are rented out on a daily or weekly basis. Addresses with good offers can be found on websites like

# From arrival to weather

**Your holiday from start to finish: the most important addresses and information for your trip to Tuscany**

www.agriturismo.org.uk, www.terranostra.it, www.agritour.net, www.agriturist.it

### BED & BREAKFAST
On the website *www.bbitalia.it* you will find numerous listings for private accommodation at attractive rates.

### CAMPING
Whether in the country, in the mountains or at the seaside, camping is still the most popular way for families to go on holidays, and the quality of Italian campsites has improved dramatically in the last few years. Whether you like it simple or prefer glamping, Tuscany is most definitely the place to go. Many campsites offer furnished self-catering holiday cabins, comfortable tents or even posh tipis with electricity and refrigerator. *www.camping.it*

### HOLIDAY ACCOMMODATION
These are some websites for you to browse prior to departure: *www.yourtuscanvilla.com, www.holidayhomestuscany.com, www.homelidays.co.uk, www.tuscany.net*

### HOTELS
In the tourist areas along the coast or in the mountains you will often only find a room with half or full board during the high season. The prices skyrocket during August. During the low season many hotels have special offers.

## ADMISSION FEES

Admission fees for museums and monuments vary widely. In the local tourist offices you can find out if there are any reduced admission tickets available and how or where you can book tickets in advance, in order to avoid long queues.

## BUDGETING

| | |
|---|---|
| Museum | from £21/$28 *online priority entrance for the Uffizi in Florence* |
| Coffee | £1.35/$1.75 *for a cappuccino at the bar counter* |
| Pizza | £7.20/$9.35 *for a pizza in a restaurant* |
| Wine | £3.60/$4.70 *for a glass of house wine* |
| Petrol | £1.50/$2.00 *for 1 litre of Super unleaded* |
| Beach | £26.95/$35.10 *per day to rent two deckchairs and an umbrella* |

## CAR & BICYCLE HIRE

Car rentals are available at all the airports and in the cities at the major companies. A credit card is obligatory. For a small car you will pay from approx. 80 euros per day, weekly rates are cheaper. Booking prior to your trip is often cheaper.

Vespa and motorcycle rental companies are also available in the major holiday resorts. The Vespa, the legendary Italian scooter, takes some getting used to. Helmets are mandatory and are generally included in the price.

There are bicycle rentals at the main train station in Florence, otherwise you can ask at your hotel or at the local tourism information.

## CARSHARING

It is the same drama everywhere: There are no parking places, the public bus service is sporadic at best and then it is still a long way to walk to the place you want to get to. Moreover, traffic has now been banned from many old town centres. But many forward-thinking towns and villages of this eco-friendly region have made life much easier for owners of electric cars. If you do car sharing, you may even be allowed in areas that are closed to normal traffic, for example into the pedestrian areas of the city centres.

There are now three places in Florence that offer car sharing: Car2go, Share'ngo (where women ride free at night), and Enjoy, which has a larger radius than the others. Carsharing Arezzo offers a range of vehicles from minibuses to one-person-cars, as does GreenGo in Pisa. Livorno, Massa and Pistoia all have their car sharing fleets or are in the process of organising them as you read this. Watch this space!

## CLIMATE, WHEN TO GO

A temperate Mediterranean climate prevails throughout Tuscany and in the winter the sun shines often, however there are also cold and especially wet days. It normally only snows in the higher regions. Spring and autumn are the best times to travel. Travelling to Tuscany in August is not ideal: the beaches are overcrowded and the cities are hot and deserted.

## CONSULATES & EMBASSIES

### BRITISH EMBASSY ROME
*Via XX Settembre 80a | I-00187 Roma RM | tel. +39 06 42 20 00 01 | ukinitaly.fco.gov.uk/en*

### US CONSULATE GENERAL FLORENCE
*Lungarno Vespucci 38 | I-50123 Florence | tel. +39 055 266951 | florence.usconsulate.gov*

### CANADIAN EMBASSY IN ROME
*Via Zara 30 | I-00198 Rome | tel. +39 06 85 44 41 | www.canadainternational.gc.ca/italy-italie*

## CUSTOMS

UK citizens do not have to pay any duty on goods brought from another EU country as long as tax was included in the price and are for private consumption. The limits are: 800 cigarettes, 400 cigarillos, 200 cigars, 1kg tobacco, 10L spirits, 20L liqueurs, 90L wine, and 110L beer.

Travellers from the USA, Canada, Australia or other non-EU countries are allowed to enter with the following tax-free amounts: 200 cigarettes or 100 cigarillos or 50 cigars or 250g tobacco, 2L wine, 2L spirits (under 22% vol.) and 1L spirits (over 22% vol.).

Travellers to the United States who are returning residents of the country do not have to pay duty on articles purchased overseas up to the value of $800, but there are limits on the amount of alcoholic beverages and tobacco products. For the regulations for international travel for U.S. residents please see *www.cbp.gov*

## DRIVING

On the motorways the maximum speed is 130 km/h or 80 mph and in suburban areas 90 km/h or 55mph. The alcohol limit is 0.5 and talking on a mobile phone whilst driving is prohibited. Outside of towns the cars dipped-beam headlamps must always be on, and in case of an accident or breakdown you have to wear a reflective vest when leaving your car. Petrol stations are open on weekdays from 7.30am to 12.30pm and 3pm to 7pm, Sundays only at certain arterial roads and along the motorways. There are self-service machines everywhere and they are usually open 24 hours. You have to pay toll on the motorways, but they are recommended for longer trips because the regional roads often run through hilly, mountainous regions and are often slow and winding. A toll road is also being planned for both the Tuscan motorways Florence–Siena–Grosseto and Florence–Pisa–Livorno.

The sign ZTL (Zona a Traffico Limitato) at the entrance to the historic downtown areas indicates that only vehicles with permission are allowed access. This applies to most vehicles in almost all the inner cities and car parks on the outskirts are expensive. If you have booked into a hotel in the old town there is usually a residential parking permit. But you may also have to move the car from the inner city after you have unloaded your luggage. Only hotels with three stars or more have private garages or parking areas. Only residents are allowed to park on the side of the road. Parking discs suffice for blue marked parking spots or else be on the lookout for parking ticket machines. For longer stays it is more convenient to use the paid parking garages and parking lots which almost every town has within close proximity of the sites (approx. 1–2 euros per hour).

If you are planning a trip to another town, it is best to use public transport where possible and the bus and the train network goes almost everywhere. But if you want to spend the evening rather take your own vehicle as there are hardly any buses or trains after 10pm.

## ELECTRICITY

The power supply complies with European Union norms standards. It is advisable to carry an adapter for the plugs.

# CURRENCY CONVERTER

| £ | € | € | £ |
|---|---|---|---|
| 1 | 1.14 | 1 | 0.88 |
| 3 | 3.41 | 3 | 2.64 |
| 5 | 5.68 | 5 | 4.40 |
| 13 | 14.76 | 13 | 11.44 |
| 40 | 45 | 40 | 35.19 |
| 75 | 85 | 75 | 65.98 |
| 120 | 136 | 120 | 105 |
| 250 | 284 | 250 | 220 |
| 500 | 568 | 500 | 440 |

| $ | € | € | $ |
|---|---|---|---|
| 1 | 0.86 | 1 | 1.17 |
| 3 | 2.57 | 3 | 3.50 |
| 5 | 4.29 | 5 | 5.83 |
| 13 | 11.15 | 13 | 15.17 |
| 40 | 34.32 | 40 | 46.67 |
| 75 | 64.35 | 75 | 87.50 |
| 120 | 103 | 120 | 140 |
| 250 | 215 | 250 | 292 |
| 500 | 429 | 500 | 583 |

For current exchange rates see www.xe.com

## EMERGENCY SERVICES

*Carabinieri* (for crime) *tel. 112;* Fire brigade *(Vigili del fuoco) tel. 115;* Emergency doctor and ambulance *tel. 118;* Police (for accidents or emergency doctor) *tel. 113* Breakdown assistance *tel. 80 31 16* (from a foreign mobile phone *8 00 11 68 00).*

## HEALTH

If you are a UK or European Union resident your free European Health Insurance Card (EHIC) will allow you access to medical treatment while travelling. If you are treated at a private practise or private clinic you have to pay upfront and then claim from your insurance on your return home. Private medical travel insurance is recommended. The hospital ambulances *(pronto soccorso)* are generally very fast and good.

## IMMIGRATION

Citizens of the UK & Ireland, USA, Canada, Australia and New Zealand need only a valid passport to enter all countries of the EU. Children below the age of 12 need a children's passport.

## INFORMATION

**ITALIAN GOVERNMENT TOURIST BOARD**
– *1 Princes St. | London W1B 2AY | tel. 020 74 08 12 54 | www.italiantourist board.co.uk*
– *630 Fifth Avenue | New York NY 10111| tel. 212 245 48 22 | www.italiantourism.com*
– *110 Yonge Street East Suite 503 | Toronto ON M5C IT4 | tel. 416 925 48 82 | e-mail: toronto@enit.it*

**WWW.TURISMO.INTOSCANA.IT**
The official website for the Tuscany region has lots of information and many links to other sites.

## INVOICES & RECEIPTS

For all services and goods you have to ask for receipts in Italy *(scontrino)* and these must be kept to show to the tax authorities *(Guardia di Finanzia)* who conduct frequent spot-checks.

## MONEY & CREDIT CARDS

Almost all the banks have ATMs or *banco-mat* and many restaurants, hotels, shops and fuel stations accept credit cards.

## MUSEUMS

The large state museums are closed on Mondays. Admission is free for EU citizens under the age of 18. For ages 18 to 25 admission is half price. In all state museums, ● admission is free on the first Sunday of the month!

## OPENING HOURS

Lunchtime is still sacred in Tuscany. Smaller shops are generally open from 9am to 1pm and then from 4pm to 7.30pm. They are also closed on Sundays and Monday mornings. Many large supermarkets and shopping centres are open from 8am to 8pm, sometimes even on Sundays. Churches are mostly closed over lunch. No sightseeing is allowed during services.

## PHONE & MOBILE PHONE

The international dialling code for Italy is *0039*; the area code is part of the number and must always be dialled (including the zero). Dial *0044* for calls from Italy to the UK and *001* from Italy to the USA. Mobile numbers start without a zero.
There are only a few public telephones that use coins. Telephone cards *(carta telefonica)* are available in bars, tobacco shops and post offices. For frequent callers it is worthwhile buying a rechargeable SIM card from one of the four service providers (Wind, Vodafone, Telecom, Fastweb). When buying a SIM you have to have proof of identity, a contact address and a mobile phone.

## POLICE

In typical Italian fashion there are several categories of police: the *Vigili* or *Polizia Municipale* are traffic police while the *Carabinieri* and *Polizia di Stato* are responsible for criminal offences. The railway police are called *Polfer* and tax investigators are the *Guardia di*

*Finanza.* They are all allowed to ask for your passport.

## PUBLIC TRANSPORT

Regional public transport is comparatively inexpensive and the intercity buses and trains are fairly punctual. They run often during the day and less frequently at night. The fast Eurostar train that connects large cities is more expensive and reservations are essential. However, you can save money by purchasing your tickets a few weeks in advance. Train tickets without reservations must be validated at the station.

From Florence the intercity bus lines go to almost all places in Tuscany. Tickets for the city bus can be bought from news-stands or in tobacco shops, for intercity buses at your departure point and in the bars near the bus stops. A surcharge of 1 euro is payable on the bus.

## SMOKING

Smoking is strictly prohibited in all public indoor places, including restaurants, bars, clubs etc. that don't have special smoking rooms. Those who violate the regulations may be fined up to 250 euros.

## TAXI

Have the hotel call a minicab for you or go directly to the taxi ranks at the airport or train stations. Prices are similar to those in the UK. You are charged extra at night.

## TIPPING

It is not common practice to tip in Italy. At the most you might want to round up the bill in a restaurant by a couple of euros. Always wait though until the waiter has brought your change before leaving your tip on the table.

# WEATHER IN FLORENCE

| | Jan | Feb | March | April | May | June | July | Aug | Sept | Oct | Nov | Dec |
|---|---|---|---|---|---|---|---|---|---|---|---|---|
| Daytime temperatures in °C/°F | 8/46 | 10/50 | 14/57 | 19/66 | 23/73 | 28/82 | 31/88 | 30/86 | 26/79 | 19/66 | 13/55 | 9/48 |
| Nighttime temperatures in °C/°F | 2/36 | 3/37 | 6/43 | 9/48 | 13/55 | 16/61 | 19/66 | 19/66 | 16/61 | 12/54 | 7/45 | 3/37 |
| Sunshine hours/day | 4 | 4 | 5 | 6 | 7 | 9 | 10 | 9 | 7 | 6 | 4 | 4 |
| Precipitation days/month | 9 | 7 | 8 | 8 | 9 | 6 | 3 | 4 | 6 | 9 | 11 | 9 |

Sunshine hours/day    Precipitation days/month

# USEFUL PHRASES ITALIAN

## PRONUNCIATION

| | |
|---|---|
| c, cc | before e or i like ch in "church", e.g. ciabatta, otherwise like k |
| ch, cch | like k, e.g. pacchi, che |
| g, gg | before e or i like j in "just", e.g. gente, otherwise like g in "get" |
| gl | like "lli" in "million", e.g. figlio |
| gn | as in "cognac", e.g. bagno |
| sc | before e or i like sh, e.g. uscita |
| sch | like sk in "skill", e.g. Ischia |
| z | at the beginning of a word like dz in "adze", otherwise like ts |

An accent on an Italian word shows that the stress is on the last syllable.
In other cases we have shown which syllable is stressed by placing a dot below the relevant vowel.

### IN BRIEF

| | |
|---|---|
| Yes/No/Maybe | Sì/No/Forse |
| Please/Thank you | Per favore/Grazie |
| Excuse me, please! | Scusa!/Mi scusi |
| May I...?/Pardon? | Posso...? / Come dice?/Prego? |
| I would like to.../Have you got...? | Vorrei.../Avete...? |
| How much is...? | Quanto costa...? |
| I (don't) like that | (Non) mi piace |
| good/bad | buono/cattivo/bene/male |
| broken/doesn't work | guasto/non funziona |
| too much/much/little/all/nothing | troppo/molto/poco/tutto/niente |
| Help!/Attention!/Caution! | aiuto!/attenzione!/prudenza! |
| ambulance/police/fire brigade | ambulanza/polizia/vigili del fuoco |
| Prohibition/forbidden/danger/dangerous | divieto/vietato/pericolo/pericoloso |
| May I take a photo here/of you? | Posso fotografar La? |

### GREETINGS, FAREWELL

| | |
|---|---|
| Good morning!/afternoon!/ evening!/night! | Buon giorno!/Buon giorno!/ Buona sera!/Buona notte! |
| Hello! / Goodbye!/See you | Ciao!/Salve! / Arrivederci!/Ciao! |
| My name is... | Mi chiamo... |
| What's your name? | Come si chiama?/Come ti chiami |
| I'm from... | Vengo da... |

# Parli italiano?

"Do you speak Italian?" This guide will help you to say the basic words and phrases in Italian

## DATE & TIME

| | |
|---|---|
| Monday/Tuesday/Wednesday | lunedì/martedì/mercoledì |
| Thursday/Friday/Saturday | giovedì/venerdì/sabato |
| Sunday/holiday/ working day | domenica/(giorno) festivo/ (giorno) feriale |
| today/tomorrow/yesterday | oggi/domani/ieri |
| hour/minute | ora/minuto |
| day/night/week/month/year | giorno/notte/settimana/mese/anno |
| What time is it? | Che ora è? Che ore sono? |
| It's three o'clock/It's half past three | Sono le tre/Sono le tre e mezza |
| a quarter to four | le quattro meno un quarto/ un quarto alle quattro |

## TRAVEL

| | |
|---|---|
| open/closed | aperto/chiuso |
| entrance/exit | entrata/uscita |
| departure/arrival | partenza/arrivo |
| toilets/ladies/gentlemen | bagno/toilette/signore/signori |
| (no) drinking water | acqua (non) potabile |
| Where is...?/Where are...? | Dov'è...?/Dove sono...? |
| left/right/straight ahead/back | sinistra/destra/dritto/indietro |
| close/far | vicino/lontano |
| bus/tram | bus/tram |
| taxi/cab | taxi/tassì |
| bus stop/cab stand | fermata/posteggio taxi |
| parking lot/parking garage | parcheggio/parcheggio coperto |
| street map/map | pianta/mappa |
| train station/harbour | stazione/porto |
| airport | aeroporto |
| schedule/ticket | orario/biglietto |
| supplement | supplemento |
| single/return | solo andata/andata e ritorno |
| train/track | treno/binario |
| platform | banchina/binario |
| I would like to rent... | Vorrei noleggiare... |
| a car/a bicycle | una macchina/una bicicletta |
| a boat | una barca |
| petrol/gas station | distributore/stazione di servizio |
| petrol/gas/diesel | benzina/diesel/gasolio |
| breakdown/repair shop | guasto/officina |

## FOOD & DRINK

| | |
|---|---|
| Could you please book a table for tonight for four? | Vorrei prenotare per stasera un tavolo per quattro? |
| on the terrace/by the window | sulla terrazza/ vicino alla finestra |
| The menu, please | La carta/il menù, per favore |
| Could I please have...? | Potrei avere...? |
| bottle/carafe/glass | bottiglia/caraffa/bicchiere |
| knife/fork/spoon/salt/pepper | coltello/forchetta/cucchiaio/sale/pepe |
| sugar/vinegar/oil/milk/cream/lemon | zucchero/aceto/olio/latte/panna/limone |
| cold/too salty/not cooked | freddo/troppo salato/non cotto |
| with/without ice/sparkling | con/senza ghiaccio/gas |
| vegetarian/allergy | vegetariano/vegetariana/allergia |
| May I have the bill, please? | Vorrei pagare/Il conto, per favore |
| bill/tip | conto/mancia |

## SHOPPING

| | |
|---|---|
| Where can I find...? | Dove posso trovare...? |
| I'd like.../I'm looking for... | Vorrei.../Cerco... |
| Do you put photos onto CD? | Vorrei masterizzare delle foto su CD? |
| pharmacy/shopping centre/kiosk | farmacia/centro commerciale/edicola |
| department store/supermarket | grandemagazzino/supermercato |
| baker/market/grocery | forno/ mercato/negozio alimentare |
| photographic items/newspaper shop/ | articoli per foto/giornalaio |
| 100 grammes/1 kilo | un etto/un chilo |
| expensive/cheap/price/more/less | caro/economico/prezzo/di più/di meno |
| organically grown | di agricoltura biologica |

## ACCOMMODATION

| | |
|---|---|
| I have booked a room | Ho prenotato una camera |
| Do you have any... left? | Avete ancora... |
| single room/double room | una (camera) singola/doppia |
| breakfast/half board/ | prima colazione/mezza pensione/ |
| full board (American plan) | pensione completa |
| at the front/seafront/lakefront | con vista/con vista sul mare/lago |
| shower/sit-down bath/balcony/terrace | doccia/bagno/balcone/terrazza |
| key/room card | chiave/scheda magnetica |
| luggage/suitcase/bag | bagaglio/valigia/borsa |

## BANKS, MONEY & CREDIT CARDS

| | |
|---|---|
| bank/ATM/pin code | banca/bancomat/ codice segreto |
| cash/credit card | in contanti/carta di credito |
| bill/coin/change | banconota/moneta/il resto |

## HEALTH

| | |
|---|---|
| doctor/dentist/paediatrician | medico/dentista/pediatra |
| hospital/emergency clinic | ospedale/pronto soccorso/guardia medica |
| fever/pain/inflamed/injured | febbre/dolori/infiammato/ferito |
| diarrhoea/nausea/sunburn | diarrea/nausea/scottatura solare |
| plaster/bandage/ointment/cream | cerotto/fasciatura/pomata/crema |
| pain reliever/tablet/suppository | antidolorifico/compressa/supposta |

## POST, TELECOMMUNICATIONS & MEDIA

| | |
|---|---|
| stamp/letter/postcard | francobollo/lettera/cartolina |
| I need a landline phone card/ I'm looking for a prepaid card for my mobile | Mi serve una scheda telefonica per la rete fissa/Cerco una scheda prepagata per il mio cellulare |
| Where can I find internet access? | Dove trovo un accesso internet? |
| dial/connection/engaged | comporre/linea/occupato |
| socket/adapter/charger | presa/riduttore/caricabatterie |
| computer/battery/rechargeable battery | computer/batteria/accumulatore |
| internet address (URL)/e-mail address | indirizzo internet/indirizzo email |
| internet connection/wifi | collegamento internet/wi-fi |
| e-mail/file/print | email/file/stampare |

## LEISURE, SPORTS & BEACH

| | |
|---|---|
| beach/bathing beach | spiaggia/bagno/stabilimento balneare |
| sunshade/lounger/cable car/chair lift | ombrellone/sdraio/funivia/seggiovia |
| (rescue) hut/avalanche | rifugio/valanga |

## NUMBERS

| | | | |
|---|---|---|---|
| 0 | zero | 15 | quindici |
| 1 | uno | 16 | sedici |
| 2 | due | 17 | diciassette |
| 3 | tre | 18 | diciotto |
| 4 | quattro | 19 | diciannove |
| 5 | cinque | 20 | venti |
| 6 | sei | 21 | ventuno |
| 7 | sette | 50 | cinquanta |
| 8 | otto | 100 | cento |
| 9 | nove | 200 | duecento |
| 10 | dieci | 1000 | mille |
| 11 | undici | 2000 | duemila |
| 12 | dodici | 10,000 | diecimila |
| 13 | tredici | ½ | un mezzo |
| 14 | quattordici | ¼ | un quarto |

# ROAD ATLAS

The green line indicates the Discovery Tour "Tuscany at a glance"
The blue line indicates the other Discovery Tours

All tours are also marked on the pull-out map

Photo: Maremma near Magliano

# Exploring Tuscany

The map on the back cover shows how the area has been sub-divided

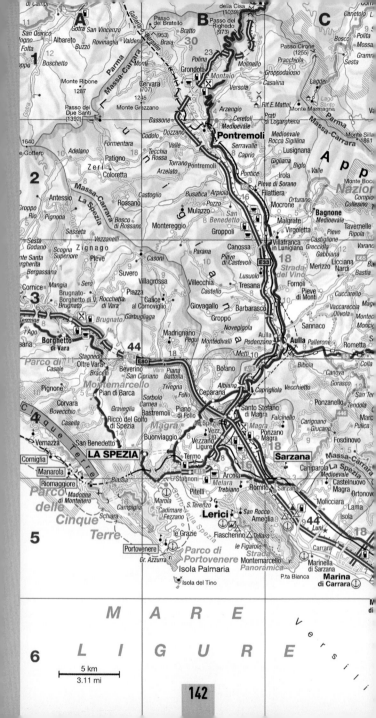

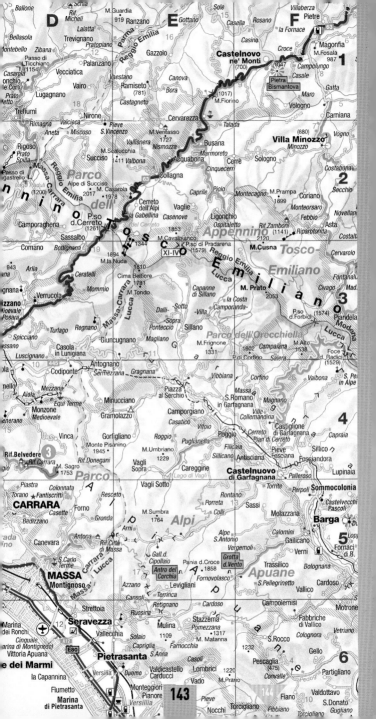

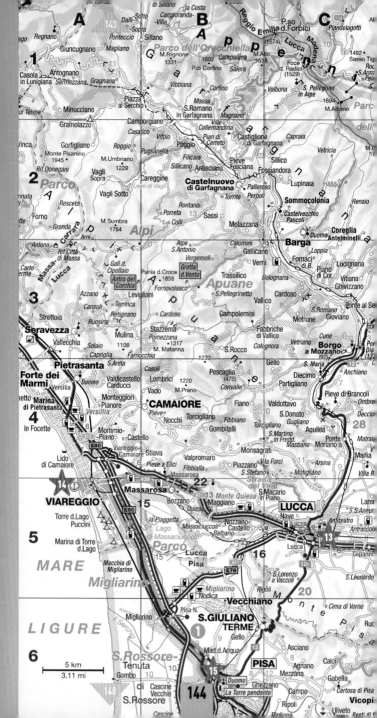

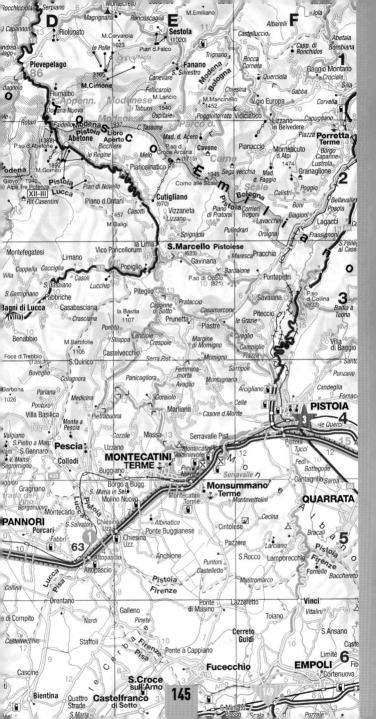

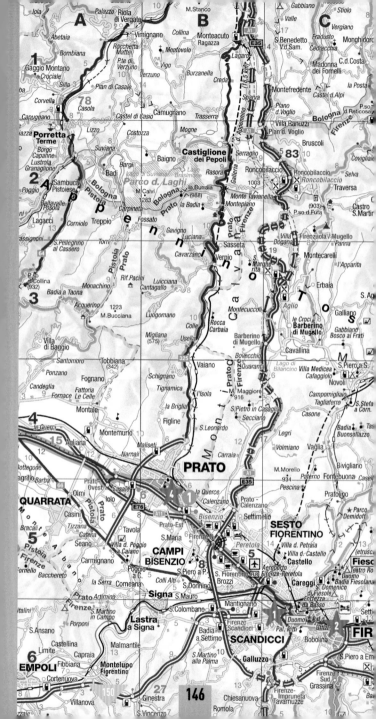

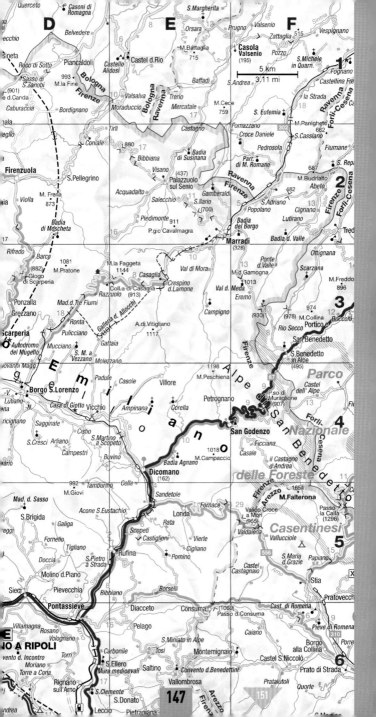

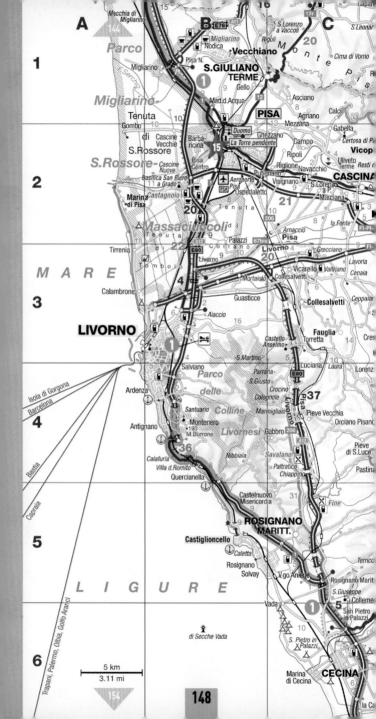

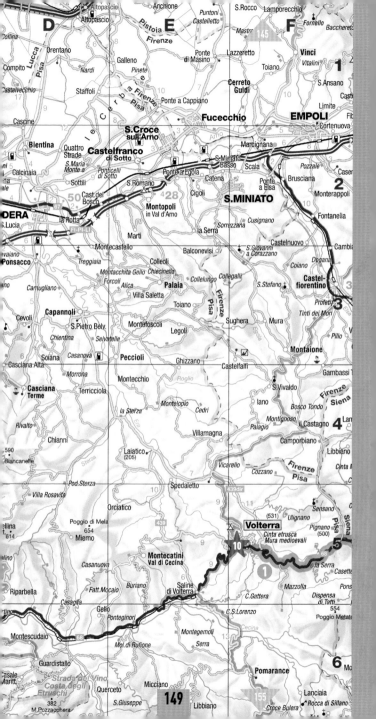

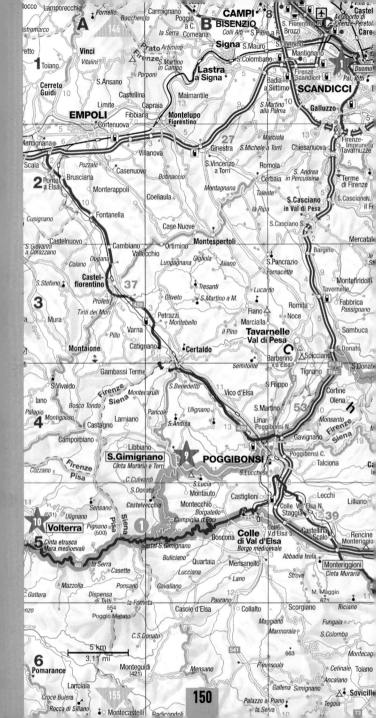

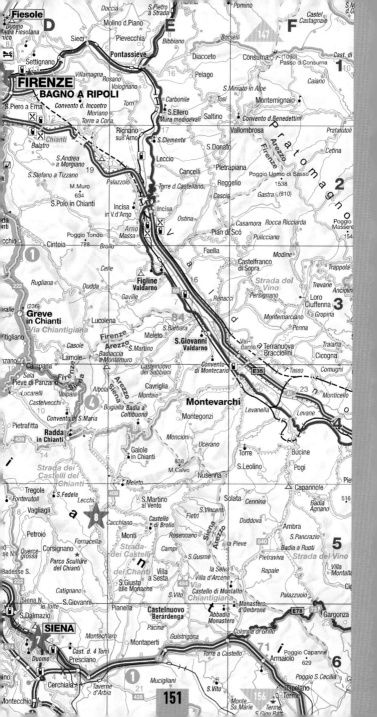

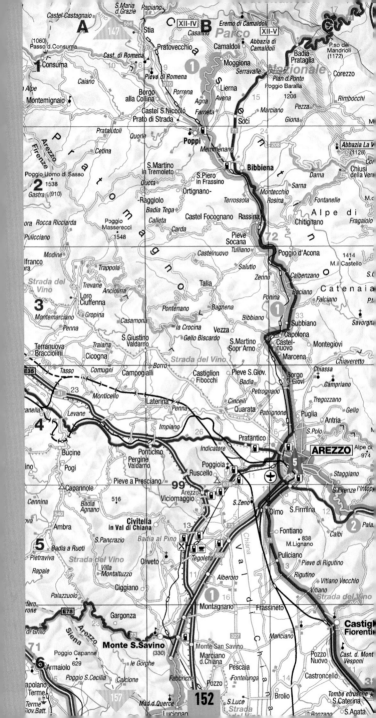

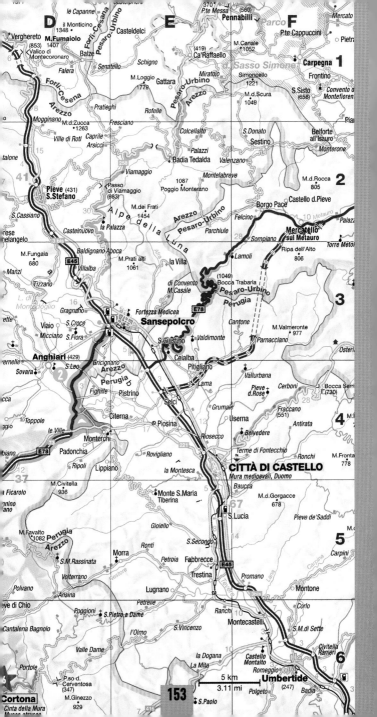

**Row 1 (D–F):**
le Capanne · il Monticino · Forli-Cesena · Casteldelci · Pte Messa (560) · **Pennabilli** · Parco · Mercato · P.te Cappuccini · Pietra

Verghereto · M.Fumaiolo 1348 · Balze · Pesaro-Urbino · M.Canale *1052 · Ca'Raffaello (419) · S.Sisto (658) · **Carpegna** · Frontino · Convento di Montefiore

(853) Valico di Montecoronaro · Falera · Senatello · Schigno · d.Sasso Simone · Simoncello 1221 · Miratoio · Pesaro-Urbino

Forli-Cesena · Arezzo · M.Loggio 1779 · Gattara · Arezzo · M.d.Scura 1049 · S.Donato · Sestino · Belforte all'Isauro · Monterone · Pia

Mogginano · M.d'Zucca *1263 · Pratieghi · Rofelle · Fresciano · Colcellalto · M.d.Rocca 805 · Castello d.Pieve

**Row 2:**
Pieve S.Stefano (431) · Ville di Roti · Caprile · Arsicci · Viamaggio · Palazzi · Badia Tedalda · Valenzano · Montelabreve · 1087 Poggio Monterano · Borgo Pace · Felcino · Mercatello sul Metauro · Palazz · Torre Mètol

S.Cassiano · Passo di Viamaggio (983) · Alpe della Luna · M.dei Frati 1454 · la Palazza · Parchiule · Sompiano · Ripa dell'Alto 806

rese ·angelo · Castelnuovo · M.Fungaia 680 · Baldignano Aboca · Villalba · M.Prati alti 1061 · la Villa · di Convento M.Casale · (1049) Bocca Trabaria · Pesaro-Urbino · Lamoli

Manzi · Tizzano · L. di · Montedoglio · Gragnano · Viaio · S.Croce · S.Fiora · Fortezza Medicea · **Sansepolcro** · S.Giustino · Cantone · Perugia · M.Valmeronte 977 · Osteri

ette · Micciura · Anghiari (429) · S.Leo · Gricignano · Arezzo · Perugia · Celalba · Valdimonte · Parnacciano

Sovara · Toppole · Fighille · Pistrino · Pitigliano · Vallurbana · Cerboni · Bocca Serr E(730)

cca · le Ville · Citerna · Selci · Lama · Grumale · Pieve d.Rose · Fraccano (551) · Antirata · M.E

ggio · Monterchi · Piosina · Userna · Belvedere · Ronchi · M.Fronta 778

biano · Padonchia · Ripoli · Lippiano · Riosecco · Terme di Fontecchio

**Row 4–5:**
a Ficarola · mnino ano · M.Civitella 936 · la Montesca · **CITTÀ DI CASTELLO** · Mura medioevali, Duomo · Baucca · M.d.Gorgacce 678 · Pieve de'Saddi

M.Favalto 1082 · Perugia · Arezzo · Monte S.Maria Tiberina · S.Lucia · M.d

S.M.Rassinata · Gioiello · Ronti · S.Secondo · Promano · Carpini

Polvano · Volterrano · Ansina · Morra · Petroia · Fabbrecce · Trestina · Montone

eve di Chio · Poggioni · S.Pietro a Dame · Lugnano · Promano

Cantalena Bagnolo · l'Olmo · Petrelle · S.Vincenzo · Ranchi · Corlo · S.M. di Sette

Portole · Valle Dame · la Dogana La Mita · Montecastelli · Civitella Ranieri

**Cortona** · Cinta della Mura · P.so d. Cerventosa · M.Ginezzo 929 · la Dogana La Mita · Castello Montalto · Romeggio · **Umbertide** · Badia · S.Paolo · Polgeto

5 km · 3.11 mi

**153**

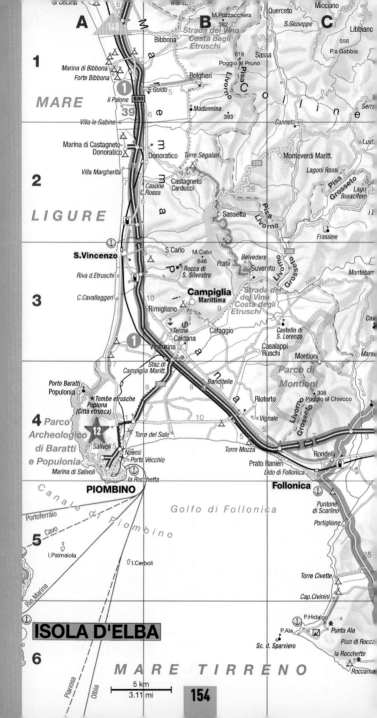

A

B

C

1

2

3

4

5

6

di Cécina
M.Pozzácchera
382
Querceto
Micciano
S.Giuseppe
Libbiano
558
P.a Gabbia
Bibbona
Strada del Vino
Costa degli
Etruschi
Sassa
619
Poggio al Pruno
Marina di Bibbona
Forte Bibbona
il Palone
E80
S.Guido
Bolgheri
Madonnina
393
39
Villa le Sabine
Canneto
MARE
Marina di Castagneto-
Donoratico
Donoratico
Torre Segalari
Monteverdi Maritt.
Lagoni Rossi
Villa Margherita
Casone
C. Rossa
Castagneto
Carducci
Sassetta
Lago
Boracifero
LIGURE
Frassine
S.Carlo
M.Calvi
646
Belvedere
S.Vincenzo
Riva d.Etruschi
Rocca di
S. Silvestro
Prata
Suvereto
Monteban
C.Cavalleggeri
Campiglia
Marittima
Strada del
Vino
Costa degli
Etruschi
Castello di
S. Lorenzo
Cas
Rimigliano
Cafaggio
Casalappi
Ruschi
Montioni
Terme
Caldana
Venturina
Mars
Parco di
Montioni
Staz. di
Campiglia Maritt.
Banditelle
308
Poggio al Chiecco
Porto Baratti
Populonia
Tombe etrusche
Puplona
(Città etrusca)
Riotorto
Vignale
Parco
Archeologico
di Baratti
e Populonia
Torre del Sale
Salivoli
Noémi
Porto Vécchio
Torre Mozza
Rondelli
Marina di Salivoli
la Rochetta
Prato Ranieri
Lido di Follonica
PIOMBINO
Follonica
Canale di Piombino
Portoferráio
Golfo di Follonica
Puntone
di Scarlino
Cavo
Portiglione
I.Palmaiola
I.Cerboli
Torre Civette
Cap.Civinini
Rio Marina
P.Hidalgo
P.Ala
Punta Ala
ISOLA D'ELBA
Sc. d. Sparviero
Pian di Rocca
la Rochette
Roccama
Pianosa
Olbia
MARE TIRRENO
5 km
3.11 mi

154

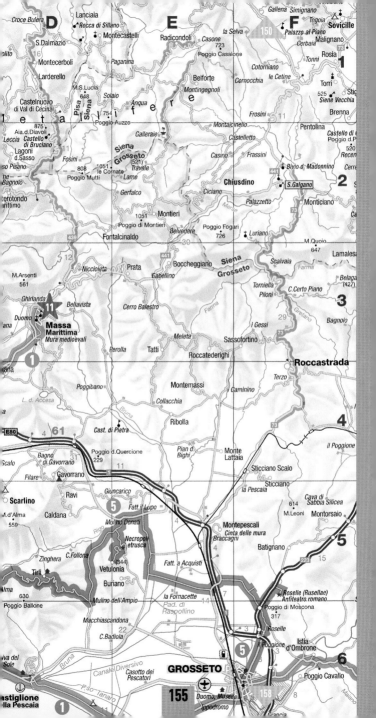

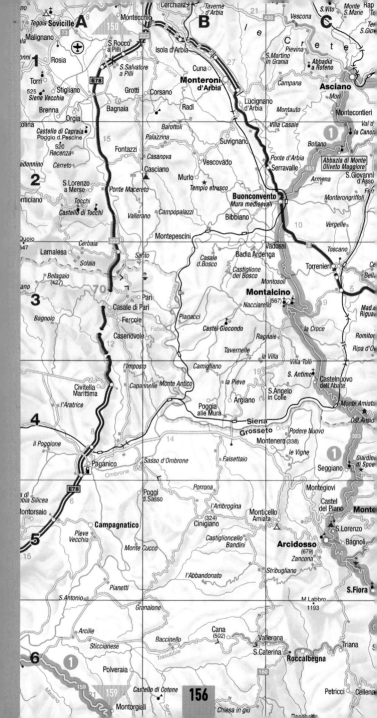

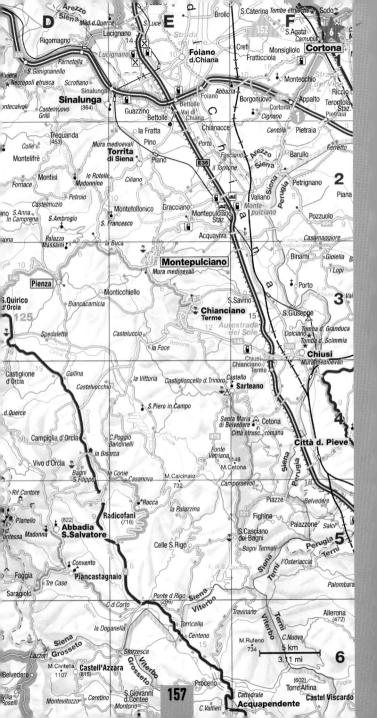

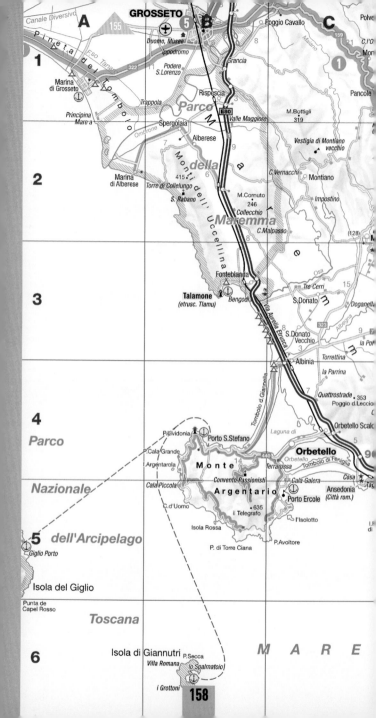

**GROSSETO**

Canale Diversivo

Pineta del Tombolo

Fso Tanara

322

Marina
di Grosseto

Principina
Mare a

Ombrone

Trappola

Podere
S.Lorenzo

Duomo, Musei
Ippodromo

Rispescia

**Parco**

Spergolaia

Alberese

Valle Maggiore

E80

Poggio Cavallo

159

Pancole

Grancia

M.Bottigli
319

Vestigia di Montiano
vecchio

C.Vernacchi

Montiano

**della**

Monti dell'Uccellina

415

Marina
di Alberese

Torre di Collelungo

S. Rabano

6

M.Cornuto
246

Collecchio

C.Malpasso

Impostino

(128)

**Maremma**

Fonteblanda

Tre Cerri

15

Talamone
(etrusc. Tlamu)

Bengodi

Via Aurelia Etrusca

S.Donato

S.Donato
Vecchio

Doganell

la Pol

323

Albegna

9

Albinia

Torrettina

la Parrina

Tombolo d.Giannella

Quattrostrade
Poggio d.Leccio

353

7

Laguna di

Orbetello Scal

5

**Parco**

P.Lividonia

Porto S.Stefano

**Orbetello**

Orbetello

Tombolo di Feniglia

9

P.Cala Grande

Argentarola

Cala Piccola

**Monte**

14

Terrarossa

Convento Passionisti

**Argentario**

635

il Telegrafo

Isola Rossa

Cala Galera

Porto Ercole

l'Isolotto

Cosa

Ansedonia
(Città rom.)

Tag

**Nazionale**

C.d'Uomo

P. di Torre Ciana

P.Avoltore

I.R.
di

**dell'Arcipelago**

Giglio Porto

**Isola del Giglio**

Punta de
Capel Rosso

**Toscana**

**M A R E**

Isola di Giannutri

P.Secca

Villa Romana

lo Spalmatoio

i Grottoni

**158**

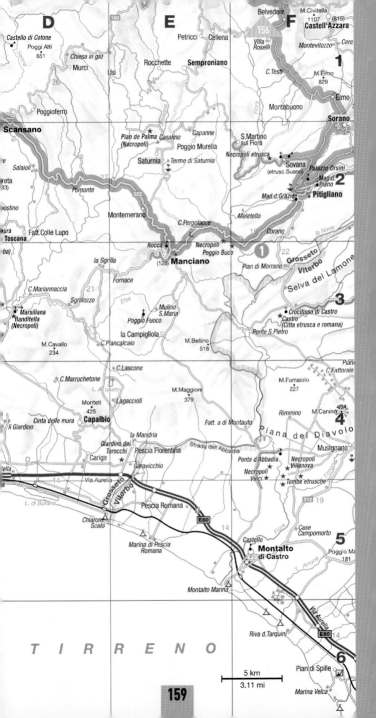

# KEY TO ROAD ATLAS

| | | |
|---|---|---|
| Autobahn mit Anschlussstelle und Anschlussnummern | Viernheim | Motorway with junction and junction number |
| Autobahn in Bau mit voraussichtlichem Fertigstellungsdatum | Datum · Date | Motorway under construction with expected date of opening |
| Rasthaus mit Übernachtung · Raststätte | Kassel · X | Hotel, motel · Restaurant |
| Kiosk · Tankstelle | | Snackbar · Filling-station |
| Autohof · Parkplatz mit WC | P | Truckstop · Parking place with WC |
| Autobahn-Gebührenstelle | | Toll station |
| Autobahnähnliche Schnellstraße | | Dual carriageway with motorway characteristics |
| Fernverkehrsstraße | | Trunk road |
| Verbindungsstraße | | Main road |
| Nebenstraßen | | Secondary roads |
| Fahrweg · Fußweg | | Carriageway · Footpath |
| Gebührenpflichtige Straße | | Toll road |
| Straße für Kraftfahrzeuge gesperrt | X X X X X | Road closed for motor vehicles |
| Straße für Wohnanhänger gesperrt | | Road closed for caravans |
| Straße für Wohnanhänger nicht empfehlenswert | | Road not recommended for caravans |
| Autofähre · Autozug-Terminal | | Car ferry · Autorail station |
| Hauptbahn · Bahnhof · Tunnel | | Main line railway · Station · Tunnel |
| Besonders sehenswertes kulturelles Objekt | ♪ Neuschwanstein | Cultural site of particular interest |
| Besonders sehenswertes landschaftliches Objekt | ✳ Breitachklamm | Landscape of particular interest |
| MARCO POLO Erlebnistour 1 | | MARCO POLO Discovery Tour 1 |
| MARCO POLO Erlebnistouren | | MARCO POLO Discovery Tours |
| MARCO POLO Highlight | ★1 | MARCO POLO Highlight |
| Landschaftlich schöne Strecke | | Route with beautiful scenery |
| Touristenstraße | Hanse-Route | Tourist route |
| Museumseisenbahn | | Tourist train |
| Kirche, Kapelle · Kirchenruine Kloster · Klosterruine | ♱ ♰ ♱ ♰ | Church, chapel · Church ruin Monastery · Monastery ruin |
| Schloss, Burg · Burgruine Turm · Funk-, Fernsehturm | ♪ ♪ ♪ ♪ | Palace, castle · Castle ruin Tower · Radio or TV tower |
| Leuchtturm · Windmühle Denkmal · Soldatenfriedhof | ♀ ✗ ⊥ ⊞ | Lighthouse · Windmill Monument · Military cemetery |
| Ruine, frühgeschichtliche Stätte · Höhle Hotel, Gasthaus, Berghütte · Heilbad | ∴ ⌂ ⌂ ♨ | Archaeological excavation, ruins · Cave Hotel, inn, refuge · Spa |
| Campingplatz · Jugendherberge Schwimmbad, Erlebnisbad, Strandbad, Golfplatz | ⚊ ⚊ △ ⚊ ☑ | Camping site · Youth hostel Swimming pool, leisure pool, beach · Golf-course |
| Botanischer Garten, sehenswerter Park · Zoologischer Garten | | Botanical gardens, interesting park · Zoological garden |
| Bedeutendes Bauwerk · Bedeutendes Areal | ■ ▢ | Important building · Important area |
| Verkehrsflughafen · Regionalflughafen | ✈ ✈ | Airport · Regional airport |
| Flugplatz · Segelflugplatz | ✈ ✈ | Airfield · Gliding site |
| Boots- und Jachthafen | ⚓ | Marina |

# MARCO POLO TRAVEL GUIDES

Travel with Insider Tips

# INDEX

This index lists all places and destinations featured in this guide.
Numbers in bold indicate a main entry.

# WRITE TO US

**e-mail: info@marcopologuides.co.uk**

Did you have a great holiday?
Is there something on your mind?
Whatever it is, let us know!
Whether you want to praise, alert us
to errors or give us a personal tip –
MARCO POLO would be pleased to
hear from you.
We do everything we can to provide the
very latest information for your trip.

Nevertheless, despite all of our authors'
thorough research, errors can creep in.
MARCO POLO does not accept any
liability for this. Please contact us by
e-mail or post.

MARCO POLO Travel Publishing Ltd
Pinewood, Chineham Business Park
Crockford Lane, Chineham
Basingstoke, Hampshire RG24 8AL
United Kingdom

**PICTURE CREDITS**
Cover photograph: Val d'Orcia (Schapowalow/SIME: M. Rellini)
Photos: DuMont picture library: Widmann (122/123, 126); Getty Images: M. Altmann (93, 128b), E. Galli (90); Getty Images/ArtMarie (19a); Getty Images/De Agostini: G. Nimatallah (94); huber-images: S. Amantini (114/115), G. Bano (57), Borchi (8), M. Borchi (17, 80), M. Carassale (2, 29, 75), Cellai (43), Cenadelli (128a), G. Cozzi (44), Dutton (10), C. Dutton (28l, 28r), O. Fantuz (12/13, 83), Gräfenhain (flap r., 61), G. Iorio (58), A. Piai (4b, 26/27), M. Rellini (37, 39, 52/53, 54/55, 117), M. Ripani (51), S. Scatà (69), Scattolin (140/141), L. Vaccarella (64); huber-images/SIME: P. Canali (30/31, 63); © iStockphoto/fatmayilmaz (18a); laif: M. Amme (120), Celentano (72), R. Celentano (9), M. Galli (31), F. Heuer (4a, 7, 70/71), A. Hub (25), M. Kirchgessner (32/33), D. Schwelle (84/85); laif/hemis.fr: P. Hauser (127); laif/robertharding: C. Kober (126/127), N. Tondini (22); Look: J. Richter (11, 67); Look/age fotostock (47); Look/ClickAlps (78); mauritius images: M. Hangen (18b); mauritius images/age fotostock: Y. Aziz (18c), A. Lebrun (30), N. Tondini (111); mauritius images/Alamy (3, 125), E. Galeotti (40), M. Glueck (20/21), G. Tagini (19b), I. Vdovin (48); mauritius images/Cultura: S. Delauw (99); mauritius images/imagebroker: B. Boensch (101), V. Wolf (34); mauritius images/Mark Bolton Photography/Alamy (6); mauritius images/Photononstop: G. Lansard (89); mauritius images/Prisma: R. Van der Meer (5, 102/103); mauritius images/Westend61: D. Simon (118/119); mauritius images/Westend61/pure.passion.photography (97); H. P. Merten (flap l); Schapowalow/SIME: M. Rellini (1a); M. Schulte-Kellinghaus (86); O. Stadler (14/15, 76/77, 129); T. P. Widmann (107)

**3rd Edition – fully revised and updated 2019**
Worldwide Distribution: Marco Polo Travel Publishing Ltd, Pinewood, Chineham Business Park, Crockford Lane, Basingstoke, Hampshire RG24 8AL, United Kingdom. Email: sales@marcopolouk.com
© MAIRDUMONT GmbH & Co. KG, Ostfildern; Chief editor: Stefanie Penck; author: Christiane Büld Campetti; co-author: Sabine Oberpriller; Picture editor: Gabriele Forst; Stefanie Wiese; Cartography road atlas & pull-out map: © MAIRDUMONT, Ostfildern; Design: milchhof : atelier, Berlin; Front cover, pull-out map cover, page 1: Karl Anders – Studio für Brand Profiling, Hamburg; Page 2/3 and Discovery Tours: Susan Chaaban, Dipl.-Des. (FH) Translated from German by Wendy Barrow, Susan Jones, Frauke Watson; editor of the English edition: Margaret Howie, fullproof. co.za; Prepress: lesezeichen verlagsdienste, Cologne; InterMedia, Ratingen; Phrase book in cooperation with Ernst Klett Sprachen GmbH, Stuttgart, Editorial by Pons Wörterbücher
All rights reserved. No part of this book may be reproduced, stored in a retrieval system or transmitted in any form or by any means (electronic, mechanical, photocopying, recording or otherwise) without prior written permission from the publisher; Printed in China

MIX
Paper from responsible sources
FSC® C124385

# DOS & DON'TS 👆

**A few things to look out on your holiday**

## DON'T BUY STAMPS AT KIOSKS

Writing postcards is seriously hip again, but watch out where you buy the stamps. Private postal services not only charge more for stamps than the post office. You will also have to write the cards there and then drop them in their own post box for it is not easily apparent which other post boxes will work for you and which won't. Best stick to the Italian post office and their red boxes!

## DON'T SNACK IN THE CITY CENTER

People having a picnic do exude a certain bucolic charm. But while this is perfectly fine in nature, in bars or public parks, it is a no-go on the steps of the Duomo or the Museum. Italians do not appreciate it at all!

## DON'T GET RIPPED OFF IN THE RESTAURANT

Do make sure to check the prices on the menu before you order your meal. Some food items, like fish or crustaceans, are often listed per etto, i.e., per 100 gram. When in doubt, consult the Italian menu and avoid restaurants where the price is not clearly shown on the menu.

## DON'T VISIT MUSEUMS SPONTANEOUSLY

Holidays are all about spontaneity, but when it comes to major museums such as the Uffizi in Florence, it pays to re- serve the tickets beforehand. Otherwise, you may waste half the day in a long queue before the ticket counter — or worse, risk being ripped off by street profiteers who sell tickets at extortionate prices.

## DON'T DISCLOSE PERSONAL DATA ONLINE

Italians love to chat. And nowadays, many Italian towns and cities provide citywide free wifi. But in Luca, Livorno and Prato, this does not work for foreign portable phones. Here, it is better to use one of the many bars offering free wifi instead of having to provide credit card details and other sensitive personal data trying to join the city network.

## DON'T GO SHOPPING IN AUGUST

Browsing the factory outlets of Gucci & Co. is part of the fun of a Tuscan visit. But keep in mind that the period around Ferragosto (15th August) is the time of their annual vacation.

## DON'T BUY KNOCK-OFFS

Bargain hunters beware: Do not be tempted to buy the oh-so reasonably priced Ray Bans, Hermes belts or Gucci handbags from the „Vu Cumpra," the friendly and voluble street vendors from Senegal or Somalia! There are frequent police checks and even you as the buyer will face a hefty fine (up to 3000 euros) for the purchase of fake luxury goods.